Portfolios Plus

Portfolios Plus

Portfolios Plus

A Critical Guide to Alternative Assessment

Linda Mabry

CORWIN PRESS, INC.
A Sage Publications Company
Thousand Oaks, California

Copyright © 1999 by Corwin Press, Inc.

For information:

 Corwin Press, Inc.
A Sage Publications Company
2455 Teller Road
Thousand Oaks, California 91320
E-mail: order@corwinpress.com

SAGE Publications Ltd.
6 Bonhill Street
London EC2A 4PU
United Kingdom

SAGE Publications India Pvt. Ltd.
M-32 Market
Greater Kailash I
New Delhi 110 048 India

Printed in the United States of America

Library of Congress Cataloging-in-Publication Data

Mabry, Linda.
    Portfolios plus: A critical guide to alternative assessment /
Linda Mabry.
        p. cm.
    Includes bibliographical references and index.

    ISBN 0-8039-6610-5 (cloth: acid-free paper)
    ISBN 0-8039-6611-3 (pbk.: acid-free paper)
    1. Educational tests and measurements—United States. 2.
Examinations—United States—Scoring. 3.
Examinations—Validity—United States. 4. Portfolios in
education—United States. I. Title.
    LB3051 .M4243   1999
    371.27—dc21
                                                        99-6169

This book is printed on acid-free paper.

99 98 99 00 01 02 03 10 9 8 7 6 5 4 3 2 1

Production Editor: S. Marlene Head
Editorial Assistant: Julia Parnell
Typesetter: Rebecca Evans
Cover Designer: Wendy Hastings Coy

CONTENTS

ACKNOWLEDGMENTS

I thank the following reviewers for their generous encouragement and suggestions:

Robert B. Amenta
California Lutheran University
Thousand Oaks, CA

Paul Gathercoal
California Lutheran University
Thousand Oaks, CA

Dorothy E. Williams
Our Lady of the Lake University
San Antonio, TX

ABOUT THE AUTHOR

Linda Mabry, designated a Spencer Fellow by the National Academy of Education, is an assessment researcher, program evaluator, and former schoolteacher. As a graduate student at the University of Illinois, she became interested in the effects of standardized testing on public education and, for her dissertation, studied an alternative to traditional tests, the Rite of Passage Experience (R.O.P.E.) at Walden III High School in Racine, Wisconsin. Since then, she has studied other teacher-developed assessment systems, developed and taught courses in performance assessment, and provided training and assistance to a variety of public schools. A current research project is an ongoing examination of state-mandated performance assessments. She is an associate with the National Center for the Improvement of Educational Assessment, a project that matches members of the measurement community and states to assist with policy and technical issues. Her research has been supported by the Spencer Foundation and the Proffitt Foundation. She has served on the faculties of education at Washington State University–Vancouver and Indiana University.

PART
ONE

Assessment, the Engine and Odometer of Reform

Contemporary education in the United States is a jumble of ideas and practices. Some complement and confirm each other; others contrast and conflict. There are simultaneous trends to centralize and to decentralize education,[1] trends to individualize instruction and to identify skills and information everyone should know, trends favoring authentic and problem-based learning and others preferring traditional academic disciplines, and trends toward and away from both standardized tests and performance assessment. Everyone is a stakeholder, whether immediate or distant, so many interests vie for dominion. Some people want to conserve what is good about education, but many are tinkerers, and some are outright revolutionaries. New policies, new laws, and new reform initiatives crowd the scene.[2]

A change here or there can have an outsized impact because of the interconnectedness of educational entities and ideas. Just as teachers affect students and students affect teachers, policy modifies practice and practice modifies policy. Professional organizations influence standards, and standards influence professional organizations. Ideas about which knowledge and skills are important imprints curriculum, and curriculum establishes and reinforces ideas about which knowledge and skills are important. Relationships engender litigation, and litigation affects relationships. A change in the role of the teacher transforms pedagogy, and a change in instructional practice transforms the role of the teacher.

Assessment has an impact on everything and everyone in the educational system.

Ours is a period of challenge. Since publication of *A Nation at Risk* in 1983,[3] reform fervor has maintained prominence in education. That education continues to hold the public's attention suggests an eagerness for improving schools, but there is simultaneous evidence that America is abandoning urban schools.[4] There are unprecedented opportunities and huge dangers. Sensitivity and insight are needed, but, unfortunately, we have more confusion than clarity. Nowhere is this more true than in assessment.[5]

Assessment has become the engine and odometer of reform. Increasingly, assessment is being used not only to monitor student achievement but also to evaluate the competence of educators and the quality of educational systems, purposes for which most standardized achievement tests were not designed. Assessment is the prime basis not only for admitting students to special programs and particular schools but also for advancing political agendae—to force restructuring, to control what is taught, to punish low-scoring students, to compel schools to comply with the mandates of policymakers.

Every person who has attended school has an opinion about how learning should be facilitated, how teachers should interact with students, and how and whether we should test and grade. Every measurement professional has a perspective on what constitutes appropriate assessment of student achievement. Often, professional discourse in the measurement community implies that long-standing theories and approaches are true, obvious, and value free rather than conceding that, like all human conceptions, they are saturated with bias. Standardized multiple-choice tests are mislabeled as objective, when they are merely scored by machines—programmed by subjective humans.

All texts about assessment manifest their authors' biases, but most do so as if offering neutral information. When a writer assumes a mantle of impartiality, he or she obstructs the reader's opportunity to identify and consider the subjectivity, bias, and advocacies that nevertheless reside in the text. This text takes as its subject assessments that differ from the traditional, so perhaps it follows that the text itself should differ by noting here and elaborating later the author's advocacy for individualized assessment of students and for the professional judgments of the teachers who, interacting with them every day, are taken to be in the best position to recognize and assess their educational progress. Let the reader take note.

That measurement theory promotes practices that empower some at the expense of others is evident in the use of test scores; in the daily conferral and denial of rewards and sanctions to students, teachers, and schools; in the public hysteria over score-based comparisons of schools, districts, states, and nations;[6] and in the competition for authority over schooling that sometimes pits educators against industry, government, and test developers. Power implications pervade the different approaches to student assessment. The traditional examination, for example, was described by Michel Foucault as "a surveillance that makes it possible to qualify, to classify, and to punish. . . . It manifests the subjection of those who are perceived as objects and the objectification of those who are subjected."[7] An assessment text should promote recognition of power issues, should provoke discussion, and thus aid understanding. Understanding is desirable, so discussion is desirable, so provocation is desirable.

Assessment should not be a closed matter but open to scrutiny and argument. A test score should not be the final statement of a student's achievement but a bit of punctuation in a continuing conversation, a question mark goading us to wonder what the score means, to ask, to look further. Learning is dynamic and ongoing, so our thinking about what a child knows should not be static. Similarly, education is dynamic and ongoing, so our thinking about measurement should not be static. Assessment paradigms and practices should not be rigid and stagnant. They should not be described in language and sign systems so technically removed that teachers and parents are unable to examine and challenge and change them. Overtechnicalization has insulated educational measurement from inspection and reconsideration for too long.

An attempt will be made here to explain in accessible language some basic assumptions that underlie different assessment systems, some connections between education and assessment, and some assessment options that have gone unrecognized. The goal is juxtaposition of approaches to support informed assessment decisions.

Notes

1. See Fuhrman and Elmore (1990).

2. See Stronach and Maclure (1996) for a description of *policy hysteria,* the introduction of new policy upon new policy in response to a problem, with no single policy implemented long enough to determine whether it would solve the problem and with multiple and conflicting policies that obstruct solution. The term is an apt description of the U.S. educational reform and testing scene.

3. National Commission on Excellence in Education (1983).

4. See Berliner and Biddle (1995) and Kozol (1992).

5. In departure from the most recent statement of Standards for Educational and Psychological Testing (draft of March 23, 1998, p. 3; www.apa.org/science/standards.html) and from others (e.g., Resnick & Resnick, 1992) who distinguish between testing and assessing, here the terms will be used synonymously as school personnel and the public typically use them.

6. See, for example, Ratnesar (1998).

7. In Rabinow (1984, p. 197).

ONE

Trends and Contexts

Learning and Measurement

What can we know about what a student has learned? Vastly different philosophies of assessment can be seen in two statements about what it is possible to know:

> Whatever exists, exists in some amount. To measure it is simply to know its varying amounts. (Edward Thorndike, 1874-1949)[1]

> Not everything that counts can be counted, and not everything that can be counted counts. (Albert Einstein, 1879-1955)

Edward Thorndike has been called the father of educational measurement. His approach to assessing student achievement presaged the educational theory known as **behaviorism**. Behaviorists define learning as change in behavior. For example, a student who did not know how to multiply would probably write down a wrong answer to the problem

$$4 \times 5 = \underline{\quad}.$$

But after learning multiplication facts, the same student would probably answer

$$4 \times 5 = \underline{\ 20\ },$$

which would represent a change in behavior. The change is quantifiable, measurable:

> number right = 0 in the first case, perhaps a pretest;

> number right = 1 in the second case, perhaps a posttest.

Education, from the perspective of Thorndike and then the behaviorists, who viewed all human behavior as stimulus and response associations,[2] is a treatment designed to change a learner's behavior. Learning has occurred when a student who responded incorrectly to a test item is able to respond correctly to the same stimulus. Educational measurement quantifies the change by assigning a number to it. The change, thus identified, can be evaluated or assessed.

In contrast to Thorndike's perspective, Einstein's words assert that much important learning cannot be directly measured; it is not quantifiable; it may not even be observable. For example, this problem with others like it

$$4 \times 5 = \underline{}$$

might elicit strong evidence that a student knows multiplication facts but only weak evidence that he or she understands multiplication. A tester could count the number of problems the student answered correctly without being able to determine whether the student understands multiplication or has merely memorized certain combinations of numbers. Education and educational measurement, in this view, are not simple matters.

Behaviorism, for which the best-known proponent was B. F. Skinner,[3] is no longer the dominant learning theory. Most educators today do not think that learning is a matter of changing behavior in response to a stimulus but a complex process, individual, and often gradual and subtle. Students may know things that do not change their behavior. An example of learning without changed behavior would be the following: A student who has merely memorized multiplication facts might answer

$$4 \times 5 = \underline{20}$$

and might give the same answer after learning that multiplication can be understood as a process of repeated addition:

$$4 + 4 + 4 + 4 + 4 = 20 \text{ or}$$
$$5 + 5 + 5 + 5 = 20.$$

In this case, an increase in knowledge would not have changed behavior. It could be argued that the test is at fault, that it failed to elicit a demonstration of the learning, that the wrong question was asked. But if Einstein was right, the problem is deeper than merely asking the right question or asking it well. Many important understandings cannot be quantified, measured, without distortion. No single test can elicit what each child knows and can do, for these are matters too subtle, multifaceted, individual, contextual, and fluid. Einstein's view contradicts a definition of learning as changed behavior and suggests instead that learning is not directly observable or measurable; it must be inferred.

An important learning theory today is **constructivism**, an idea that resonates with writings of such important educators as John Dewey,[4] Jean

Piaget,[5] and Lev Vygotsky[6] and with one of the big ideas in cognitive psychology during the past century, schema theory.[7] Constructivists believe that each person constructs his or her knowledge base, interpreting new information against a background of personal experience, values, and prior knowledge. What a person knows might be described as a mental organization of cognitive schemata, similar to a filing system with routines for retrieving and processing information. From this perspective, education is not changing a student's response to a stimulus but rather arranging conditions so the student can understand and remember new information and can construct and connect schemata.

Schema theorists have suggested that learning occurs in three ways.[8] First and easiest, new information may be merely added to a preexisting schema, a process called **accretion**. For example, a child who has a dog for a pet encounters another dog and mentally adds the second dog to his schema for dog. But grasping new information is sometimes harder, requiring changing or **tuning** a schema. For example, a child with a spaniel meets someone who has a poodle and learns that a poodle, too, is a dog but a different kind of dog. To the child's schema for dog, the idea that there are different species is added.

Learning some new information is more challenging, requiring **restructuring**. For example, a child learns that dogs belong to a larger category, animals, which includes other four-footed creatures such as cats and cows and even creatures as various as birds and fish; that animals are distinguishable from vegetables and minerals; and that even the experts are stumped as to what species some things are. Understanding may require restructuring, which may involve developing subschema, creating a mental network indicating the relationships among the schemata and among the members of a schema, and developing criteria for determining whether something belongs to one schema or another.

Perhaps an example of restructuring would be distinguishing between behaviorism and constructivism. Is behaviorism sufficient for explaining our actual experiences of the complexity and diversity of human learning? What about the learning I, myself, have done but not discussed or acted on, or not explained well, or not demonstrated on an assignment or test? What about people who emerge from the same experience or course of study expressing noticeably different ideas and behaviors? Because constructivism better accounts for the many individual variations in learning that are readily observable, many educators have made a paradigm shift from behaviorism to constructivism, a restructuring of their cognitive schemata for learning.

Constructivists think that, because each person is different, because each person's experiences are different, and because each person's background knowledge is different, each person will understand the world— or particular information—from an individual perspective. Although people can communicate and often agree because of having had similar experiences, each person's knowledge is unique. Our ability to communicate is also helped by the fact that much of what a person knows is socially constructed:[9] individually understood but learned within and from a social group with a shared frame of reference and value system.

An example of socially constructed knowledge is as follows: Although few citizens of our country have personal experience of living in a monarchy, most know how a monarchy operates because our society values our knowing and expects schools to teach about different forms of government, emphasizing our own. Because a person may apply for citizenship in countries having different forms of government but few of our countrymen do so, it appears that most of us also learn to prefer our own representative democracy. People learn about many things through others rather than through direct experience, often gaining a shared perspective on the information and a shared preference.

If each person constructs knowledge uniquely, then each student in a classroom will understand material presented to all somewhat differently, depending on his or her background knowledge, readiness to learn, interest and motivation, and other factors. Each student's achievement will be singular. Constructivist educators are likely to speak of individual differences, of a variety of learning styles, of multiple intelligences,[10] of students as active rather than passive learners, and of themselves as facilitators or coaches[11] rather than teachers. They are likely to try to individualize learning and to reject direct instruction or the idea that one curriculum is right for all students.[12]

Such ideas resonate in the history of education and testing. Individualized learning was championed by those in the child study movement, circa 1880-1914, and by progressive educators, circa 1910-1940, who also promoted experiential learning and wanted testing reform. The most renowned among them, John Dewey, wrote of "the moral standard, by which to test the work of the school upon the side of what it does directly for individuals."[13] Early examples of individualized education include Maria Montessori's Children's Houses in Italy, Margaret Naumberg's Walden School in New York, A. S. Neill's Summerhill in England, Carleton Washburne's Winnetka Plan in Illinois, and E. F. O'Neill's Prestolee School in northern England. Organizations established to promote "the freest and fullest development of the individual"[14] included the New Education Fellowship (1914), which became the World Education Fellowship (1966), and the Progressive Education Association (1919), which became the American Education Fellowship (1944-1953) and dissolved in 1955.[15]

The early purpose of assessment was prediction, the selection of appropriate candidates for particular treatments, assignments, and educational opportunities.[16] Alfred Binet's work in developing tests of general intelligence, introduced in 1905, were intended to identify developmentally disabled children in Paris to provide them with remedial education. The Army alpha and beta tests of World War I were used to match recruits, the literate and illiterate respectively, to military assignments. Soon thereafter, academic achievement tests were developed and standardized, gaining quick popularity partly because of their efficiency. By 1921, Thorndike was writing,

> Clearly defined units of measure and instruments by which to count them [have been] lacking. The first steps to establish such units of educational products, and to devise instruments to measure them with reasonable precision were taken about a dozen years ago. . . . While scientific workers in education have been establishing units and scales of educational achievement, the psychologists have been improving their tests of intelligence. . . . Measurements of pupils' capacities and achievements in more or less standardized psychological and educational units are now a common feature of elementary schools. At least a million boys and girls, probably, were measured last year in respect to general intellectual capacity for school work. The number of such measures of reading, writing, spelling, arithmetic, history, and geography made during the year probably exceeded two millions.[17]

Psychologists were interested in measurements that might contribute to identifying stages and variations in human development. Because of their capacity to identify individual differences, the tests also appealed to educators interested in experiential learning and encouragement of children's individual talents. Some hoped testing would remedy teacher error and bias in grading and their heavy consequences to students. Thorndike, for instance, denounced grades as

> opinions rather than measurements, and subject to two notable defects. Nobody could be sure what was measured, or how closely the mark or grade tallied with the reality.[18]

A half century before, Horace Mann had also worried about unsound grading. He saw education as a strategy for promoting meritocracy: "Education then, beyond all other devices of human origin, is a great equalizer of the conditions of men, the balance wheel of the social machinery."[19] Trustworthy examination results were critical to the effort. He reasoned that, compared to then-popular oral examinations by teachers, standardized testing would be more thorough, more available for public scrutiny, more indicative of instructional quality, and most of all, more impervious to assessors' personal biases and favoritism. A hundred and fifty years later, the thoroughness of the tests has been questioned by those who say testing narrows curricula and focuses on factual recall rather than understanding; judicial intervention has been required to penetrate test security; program evaluators have warned against overreliance on test scores as indicators of educational quality; and the tests stand accused of a variety of biases.

In dissonance with individualized education, standardized testing has pushed us toward uniformity, assessing all in a group of test-takers on the same content[20] and in the same formats, administered under the same conditions, completed in the same time limits, each student's performance compared to the same standard. Aligned with the tests, many educational policies and practices suggest an underlying theory of learning in which information needs are largely the same and learning styles more alike than unalike. Curriculum guidelines, goals, and learning outcomes—now ubiquitous at national, state, and local levels—all imply that students should learn the same things. Partly because of the strong influence of assessment on curriculum, many of today's schools offer students more or less the same topics in more or less the same sequences—standardized learning as a consequence of standardized assessment.

Insensitive by design to what students have actually learned, to the curricula they have actually experienced, standardized testing presumes similarity of educational content across classrooms. The idea that all students should learn the same content ignores not only individualizing ideas like progressivism and constructivism but also the tradition of education in the United States, which has long been an extraordinarily variegated enterprise with many different curricula and many different pedagogies. Undercutting both countervailing theory and local innovation,[21] the presumption of uniformity has been operationalized: test developers publicly release sample and practice items; a test preparation industry has grown up offering information, classes, and self-help materials;[22] and educators who gradually develop familiarity with particular tests over time, pressed by stakes as high as job loss for themselves and denial of diplomas for their students, make adjustments. Curriculum is narrowed to test content; pedagogy is distorted into "multiple-choice teaching"; instructional time is lost to test practice preparation.[23] Test scores are the coin of the educational realm pressing teachers, students, and the educational system into conformity.

The negative effects of large-scale, standardized, norm-referenced, multiple-choice testing were not intended by early testing proponents, but deleterious consequences were predicted from the outset. Vigorous in "the effort to replace opinion by measurement,"[24] Thorndike countered three early criticisms of the new science of educational measurement raised by objectors. Of the prescient worry that scores would become an end in themselves, he wrote,

> First, it will be said that learning should be for learning's sake, that too much attention is given already in this country to marks, prizes, degrees and the like, that students work too much for marks rather than for real achievement. . . . Students will work for marks and degrees if we have them. We can have none, or we can have such as are worth working for. Either alternative is reasonable, but the second seems preferable.[25]

Many now think that higher test scores "are worth working for" but, in a reversal of Thorndike's meaning, because low scores bring humiliation and severe punishment. To many, high-stakes testing seems neither "reasonable" nor "preferable."

Of the premonition that teachers might be diverted from teaching into test preparation, Thorndike argued,

> It will be said that the energy of teachers should be devoted to making achievements great rather than to measuring how great they are. . . . Most of us need to know what we are trying to teach or learn, and how far we have taught it or learned it; and will be aided, not hindered, by instruments for measuring educational purposes and products.[26]

Not only "the energy of teachers" but also instructional time and educational resources, including funding estimated at half to three quarters of a billion dollars annually,[27] have been diverted to testing rather than learning. Whether education has, on balance, been "aided, not hindered, by instruments for measuring" is a matter of open controversy.

In response to the foresight that important educational goals and objectives might languish in a pro-testing environment, Thorndike pleaded,

> It will be said that only the baser parts of education can be counted and weighed, and that the finer consequences for the spirit of man will be lost, in proportion as we try to measure them, . . . but I beg you to believe that the fear is groundless.[28]

The tests, especially now standards-based assessments, are still popular. But "groundless" or not, the fear that "the finer consequences for the spirit of man will be lost, in proportion as we try to measure them" remains. Today's testing critics are better informed by empirical evidence of test-engendered problems; test developers are armed with more carefully honed technical procedures; the public is ever more insatiable for simple, comparative, bottom-line indicators of educational quality, for test scores.

High-stakes minimum-competency tests spread rapidly throughout the United States during the 1970s,[29] followed by the state testing programs now in place in all but one state,[30] followed by development of national standards[31] and calls for a national test.[32] Increasingly, large-scale educational reform efforts have emphasized accountability—and accountability initiatives have prioritized standardized test scores as indicators of educational quality.[33]

When test scores carry high stakes, such as student eligibility for special programs or graduation and teacher or administrator evaluation, they have a strong impact on educational systems and the people in them. Pressure is strong on students who will be denied privileges if their scores are low, on teachers who may lose their standing or their jobs if the students

Figure 1.1 Stress Test

NOTE: This cartoon about Indiana's state test, the Indiana Statewide Testing for Educational Progress (ISTEP+), was created by middle school student Scott Kerlin and printed in his school newspaper, *Somewhere in the Middle*, Rensselaer, Indiana, May 1998. (Reprinted by permission of S. Kerlin and parents.)

assigned to them do not score well, and on administrators whose schools or districts suffer public humiliation in the news media or lose autonomy if their aggregated scores are not as high as in other schools or districts. A middle school teacher in rural Pennsylvania lamented as she laid out materials for her state's English-language arts test,

> This test is not really a fair representation of how well my students can write. They could do better if they had a choice of topics and

could do the sorts of things we usually do [in class]. . . . I'm frustrated. We've done all this preparation and I've organized to the max so they can concentrate on their writing during the test time, but my students will still score at only about the state average. We're a rural district, and we don't have all the curricular options and resources you find some places. . . . But my students will be compared to students who are in suburban schools with a writing-only curriculum. When the scores are printed in the newspaper, people will think we're not doing a good job of teaching here. It just doesn't seem fair.[34]

Pressures are strong even in situations where stakes are thought to be low, for example, where students are not denied diplomas or where teachers are not evaluated on the basis of test scores. For example, a Michigan principal said of the state's 1998 High School Proficiency Test, scores from which were reported in local newspapers, although diplomas did not depend on scores,

There's just no reason for the kids to do well. If a few blow it off, statistically you're dead. I'm anticipating a big disaster. . . . The charts and graphs, the numbers are what people look at. If I try to explain the scores, the public will think it's an excuse. . . . Testing is a political football in Michigan. We're stuck in the middle, getting kicked around.[35]

Is testing fair to students, to teachers, to schools? Practices perceived as promoting equity in assessment necessarily differ depending on the perspective taken regarding individualized understandings and common knowledge. In individualized education—whether the impulse arises in progressive education, alternative schooling, or constructivist learning theory—test-takers are understood to have different achievements, different learning styles, and different response styles. Different test content and formats are needed if each test-taker is to demonstrate learning to the best of his or her ability. From this viewpoint, treating students as if they were identical when they clearly are not, as if their learning opportunities were identical when they clearly are not, is unfair. By contrast, in standardized, norm-referenced testing, different test content or response formats seem unfair. Everything about the test must be the same, must be equal, for comparisons based on test scores to be fair.

Test scores facilitate comparisons among large numbers of students better than classroom grades. Comparisons of scores can indeed be helpful for matching students' educational needs to available resources, providing reference points in understanding students' achievements relative to their age-mates, and identifying individual progress and general trends over time.

TABLE 1.1 A Brief Assessment Timeline

2000 B.C.	Chinese civil service exams were established in a move toward meritocracy and away from unfair preference in choosing civil servants.
400 B.C.	Socrates in Athens, Greece developed conversational methods to assess the positions described and defended rhetorically by students.
1700s	Early U.S. testing involved oral examinations conducted by faculty who used professional judgment to determine the quality of student performances.
1830s	Horace Mann first used written tests in Massachusetts and Connecticut. Mann championed standardization to curb unfairness and bias in grading. Mann's 1846 Boston Survey was the first printed test for large-scale assessment of student achievement in geography, grammar, history, philosophy, astronomy, writing, and arithmetic. The Boston School Committee was shocked by low student performance. Because tests results were unused, they were discontinued in 1847.
1895	Joseph Rice conducted testing in a number of large school systems. Results: (1) negligible differences in spelling scores regardless of amount of instruction time, and (2) large differences in math scores among schools. Recommendation: standardize examinations.
1900s	Alfred Binet developed tests of general intelligence (g), to identify developmentally disabled children in Paris and to provide them with remedial education. Edward Thorndike, "father of educational measurement," worked tirelessly to devise and promote objective tests to improve on classroom assessments. The U.S. Army's alpha and beta tests, for literate and illiterate World War I recruits, were used to match personnel to military assignments. By the 1920s, standardized, norm-referenced tests began to be widely implemented.
1933-1941	The Progressive Education Association emphasized the ideas of John Dewey and others regarding individualized, experiential education. Ralph Tyler's Eight-Year Study in 300 colleges and universities of students from 30 high schools associated with progressive education found that the students outperformed matched peers ($n = 1,475$) who had been exposed to rigid college-preparatory curricula.
1957	The successful launching of the first satellite, Sputnik I, by the USSR generated intense desire in the United States to outperform Cold War competitors. Political momentum swelled for developing better instructional programs, especially in science and technology, and for comparing educational results internationally.
1965	The Elementary and Secondary Education Act (ESEA) of 1965 was passed, "new math" and other curricular and pedagogical innovations initiated, and educational evaluation established to study the effectiveness of the new programs.
1969	The National Assessment of Educational Progress (NAEP), promoted by Tyler and mandated by Congress, began to chart trends in student achievement using matrix-sampled tests. Directed by the National Center for Educational Statistics (NCES), constructed-response items were included

TABLE 1.1 Continued

	in 1988. In 1990-1991, trial state assessments were first conducted. Federal law named the National Assessment Governing Board (NAGB), a group of representatives of public and educational constituencies, as the NAEP policy-setting body. NAEP increasingly influenced state assessment programs. By 1998, the Educational Testing Service (ETS) and National Computer Systems (NCS), private enterprises, were heavily involved in NAEP.
1970s	Standardized, norm-referenced (NRT), minimum-competency tests were adopted in many states and districts across the United States. Subsequently, concerns arose about teaching to the minimum, and drop-out rates increased.
1980s	Use of criterion-referenced tests (CRTs) grew in reaction to problems with NRTs, as did emphasis on educational excellence and higher-order thinking skills. Opposition to standardized testing grew, but so did the public popularity of the tests. Publication of *A Nation at Risk* (National Commission on Excellence in Education, Washington, DC: Government Printing Office) in 1983 ushered in a new round of educational panic and reform fervor, which remained unabated for 15 years. Reform focused not on curricular improvement but on accountability, with aggregated scores on standardized achievement tests the prime indicator of educational quality.
1990s	Testing dominated educational reform despite substantial research documenting problems with standardized tests, including biases, distortion of curriculum, and diversion of resources from instruction to testing. As alternatives to standardized multiple-choice tests, performance assessments were developed locally and by states. The National Council of Teachers of Mathematics (NCTM) developed well-received standards, leading to the development of standards in other subjects by other organizations. States moved into standards-based assessment. Conservative opposition, centered on cost and privacy issues, effected retreats from performance assessment in some states.
1994	Improving America's Schools Act (IASA) mandated national biennial assessment of individual students (full census tests, not matrix sampling) and charged NAGB with determining which subjects to test, performance standards, instruments, and reporting results. A new national system of assessments, to include performance items, was to be voluntary.
1994	GOALS 2000: Educate America Act established national educational goals requiring that, by the year 2000: (1) all children will have access to preschools that prepare them for school; (2) 90% of students will complete high school; (3) all students will demonstrate competence in prescribed subjects in grades 4, 8, and 12; (4) all teachers will have access to professional development; (5) U.S. students will be first in the world in achievement in math and science; (6) all adults will be literate and able to compete in a global economy; (7) all schools will be free of drugs, alcohol, and violence; and (8) every school will promote parental participation in children's development and education.

It has become common to find that pressure has led to teaching to the test, rearranging school time for test preparation at the expense of the curriculum, and keeping low-scoring students from testing so as to raise a school's aggregated scores. Even educators who have resisted pressure to distort content and learning processes to raise scores worry: If we teach to the test, do we deny our students the best possible education? If we don't teach to the test, will our students get lower scores and be denied important opportunities? Will our school be embarrassed? Will I lose prestige or be reprimanded?

Do the tests give us important information, important enough that we should tolerate these negative consequences? The continuing popularity of the tests suggests policymakers and the public would answer yes. Many educators would say no. The tests have been challenged as biased against some students, rather than giving accurate and useful information. For example, in the first legal decision that standardized tests discriminate against any group, a suit brought by American Civil Liberties Union Women's Rights Project, New York state's method of granting merit scholarships based on SAT scores was ordered changed by federal judge John M. Walker in Manhattan, who stated,

> After a careful review of the evidence, this court concludes that SAT scores capture a student's academic achievement no more than a student's yearbook photograph captures the full range of her experiences in high school.[36]

Many teachers find the tests do not tell them much about what their students have learned; information from their own classrooms is typically more detailed and useful.[37]

Some teachers have developed outstanding assessment practices on the basis of their professional experience and devotion to their students. But even teachers who have developed assessments more appropriate for teaching and learning and more capable of supporting valid inferences of student achievement than the tests are effectively shut out of many of the consequential discussions about assessment. The examples of teacher-developed assessments in Part 2 demonstrate how testing could be enriched by the ideas of educators. One purpose for this volume is to help them gain an entre to the grand conversation in educational measurement.

New Assessment Methods

The 1990s became a period of experimentation with a variety of assessment techniques as teachers sought better means for recognizing student learning. Teachers have always assessed students' performances, always done performance assessment, so some of the "new" methods are continuations or revisions of long-standing practice. These methods, as a group, have sometimes been called **alternative assessment** to distinguish them from standardized testing and have also been called

- **authentic assessment** when test problems resemble the kinds of tasks undertaken by professionals, that is, when test questions are authentic to the so-called real world outside of schools;[38]

- **direct assessment** when test-takers are asked to demonstrate the skill of interest, for example, in an assessment of writing, to write rather than to answer multiple-choice items about vocabulary or grammar serving as proxies for the skill of writing; and

- **performance assessment** when test-takers are asked to perform or demonstrate skills either by doing something that is observed and evaluated as it occurs (e.g., a debate or a musical concert) or by doing something that results in a tangible product that can be evaluated (e.g., a sculpture or a working model).

What these umbrella terms have in common is the requirement for **constructed-response** rather than *selected-response* test questions or items.[39] That is, test-takers cannot simply select an answer from among two, four, or five response options but must construct a response of their own. There are a variety of types of constructed responses, including the following.

- **PORTFOLIO:** a collection of information by and about a student to give a broad view of his or her achievement. A portfolio contains samples of student work in one or more areas. It may also contain narrative descriptions, grades or other evaluations by teachers and others, official records, student reflection or self-evaluation, responses from parents, suggestions for future work, and audio or photographic records.[40]

- **PROFILE:** a collection of ratings, descriptions, and summary judgments by teachers and sometimes by the student and others to give a broad view of his or her achievement. A profile typically includes a variety of contents, which may vary from checklists to certificates to narrative descriptions of what a student knows and can do. It may document academic achievement, nonacademic achievement, or both. A profile differs from a portfolio in not including samples of a student's work.[41]

- **PERFORMANCE TASK:** a task, problem, or question that requires students to construct (rather than select) responses and may also require them to devise and revise strategies, organize data, identify patterns, formulate models and generalizations, evaluate partial and tentative solutions, and justify their answers.[42]

- **PROJECT:** a specialized, often interdisciplinary inquiry devised and undertaken by a student or group of students. Project work results in personalized (and perhaps new) knowledge, idiosyncratic competencies, subtle skills, and professional-like motivation and habits.[43]

- **DEMONSTRATION (OR EXHIBITION) OF MASTERY:** often a formal, more or less public performance of student competence and skill that provides an opportunity for a summative[44] or final assessment. Demonstrations may also be formative, ongoing, informal, and embedded in curricula and everyday practice. Performances may be supported by tangible products, results of experiments, or solutions to practical problems.[45]

- **DISCOURSE ASSESSMENT:** evaluation of what a student tells about what he or she knows. Typically by talking with an assessor, the student indicates what he or she has learned, offering evidence of critical thinking or problem solving by producing narratives, arguments, explanations, original summaries, interpretations, analyses, or evaluations. The assessor listens and probes for evidence of achievement, such as responses that integrate relevant and important knowledge within a particular field and that adapt and apply knowledge to novel problems or situations.

- **SIMULATION:** a task designed to incorporate problem-solving features similar to those found in practical or professional contexts. Simulations vary in the degree to which they mirror real-life situations and in the degree to which they offer structured or ill-defined tasks. Simulations may involve role-playing, as in medical training where standardized patients simulate symptoms and score medical students on their diagnostic and other skills or computer delivery of tasks.[46]

Authentic, direct, and performance assessment *can* be standardized rather than an alternative to standardization. For example, test-takers can be required to write an essay for which all are given the same question or prompt, the same time limit, and the same access or inaccess to reference materials or computers. New techniques *can* be used in old ways. Or new assessment techniques can be curriculum based (rather than insensitive to curriculum) and individualized (rather than standardized). New methods of assessing student achievement break from tradition in different ways, and some are more nontraditional than others.

How new are new methods of assessing student achievement? There are important differences between new and traditional approaches to assessing student achievement and also some important differences among new assessment approaches. Three different approaches to assessment will be discussed: the so-called psychometric paradigm, the contextual paradigm,[47] and the personalized paradigm (in Chapter 2).[48] Also discussed will be purposes of assessment (in Chapter 3), different ways to score new types of assessment (in Chapter 4), and some measurement principles by which to judge the appropriateness and quality of both traditional and nontraditional assessment methods (in Chapter 5).

Teachers as Assessors

Assessment is not a new task for teachers, who make daily decisions about student achievement. It is an inevitable part of every school day: How well is Jody reading and understanding that book? What does Charlie need help with—is it calculation he's still having trouble with or translating word problems into equations? Should I show Carla how to set up that experiment, or is she at a point where she can figure it out herself? Does the class understand basic sentence structure well enough to learn about adjectives and adverbs? Formally and informally, for individuals and for groups of students, teachers continually assess their students' progress and achievements. Teachers report accomplishment to the students, their parents, and the school system by means of grades and comments written on assignments, conversations as they help students work, classroom discussions, parent-teacher conferences and casual chats, report cards, and narratives for cumulative folders.

All measurement that involves inference, such as the indirect measurement of achievement in contrast to the direct measurement of height, is susceptible to error. Error in teacher judgment is a prime reason for our century-long distrust of teachers, but the tests we have turned to as an alternative are also susceptible to error, less obvious error. Which is better: the assessments made by teachers who know their students, teachers who are subject to biases because of their personal characteristics and relationships with students, or assessments made by machines or remote scorers who know nothing of the students and who can take into account nothing of their personal circumstances and progress? Although error in teacher judgment is a known phenomenon, classroom assessments are not as bad as Thorndike charged in 1921:

> In the elementary schools we now have many inadequate and even fantastic procedures parading behind the banner of educational science. Alleged measurements are reported and used which measure the fact in question about as well as the noise of the thunder measures the voltage of the lightning.[49]

The multiple measures that teachers take across time—many tests and assignments, observations of progress as students work individually and collectively at different tasks and in different settings—provide detailed evidence for judgments of achievement. This strong evidentiary base can yield more valid inferences of student achievement than one-shot standardized tests yield.

Understanding terms, principles, and options is important for teachers and for the measurement professionals whose work should support them. Teachers are increasingly expected to develop new assessment methods and to select assessment materials skillfully. Standards for Teacher Competence in Educational Assessment of Students were jointly developed by the American Federation of Teachers, the National Council on Measurement in Education, and the National Education Association in 1990, stating that teachers should be skilled in

- choosing appropriate assessment methods;
- developing appropriate assessment methods;
- administering, scoring, and interpreting assessment results;
- using assessment results in making decisions about students, instruction, curricula, and schools;
- valid grading;
- communicating assessment results to students, parents, other educators, and other audiences; and
- recognizing unethical, illegal, and inappropriate assessment methods.[50]

In addition, the Code of Professional Responsibility in Educational Assessment was formulated in 1995 by the National Council on Measurement in Education and the American Educational Research Association.

Despite these increased expectations, teachers are rarely offered rigorous and useful training in assessment.[51] Few programs of undergraduate education for prospective teachers include a course in measurement, and most graduate courses strongly emphasize traditional measurement, which has relatively little utility for classroom teachers. Where new methods are offered to teachers, many publications and professional development workshops and training sessions offer a smorgasbord of appealing ideas and activities but fail to provide sound or coherent measurement information. As a result, there is much confusion in current attempts to improve classroom assessment.

Notes

1. Thorndike (1921, p. 379).
2. Connell (1980, p. 298).
3. Skinner (1931, 1938).
4. See Dewey (1916).
5. See Piaget (1955).
6. See Vygotsky (1978).
7. For an historical review of developments leading to the formulation of schema theory, see Bransford (1979).
8. Rumelhart and Norman (1978).

9. Vygotsky (1978).

10. The developer of the term and primary proponent of multiple intelligences is Howard Gardner (see especially 1983).

11. The notion of teachers as coaches has been elaborated in the writings of Grant Wiggins (see 1993, 1998).

12. The idea that all U.S. students should be taught a common curriculum has been espoused, for example, in Bloom (1987), Hirsch (1987), and Schlesinger (1993).

13. Dewey (1909, p. 53).

14. Connell (1980, p. 271).

15. For fuller treatment of educational trends regarding individualization and testing, see Connell (1980).

16. Unfortunately, testing has also served elitist educational agendae, functioning as part of a social "sorting machine" (Spring, 1976) for the purposes of maintaining and reproducing social class structures (Connell, 1980, p. 298). Testing has also been a tool of interest for 20th-century eugenicists desiring to prove racial, ethnic, and class superiority.

17. Thorndike (1921, pp. 373-374).

18. Thorndike (1921, p. 372).

19. Mann (1848; see http://www.tncrimlaw.com/civil_bible/horace_mann.htm).

20. However, some new computer-generated tests offer different sets of items to each test-taker.

21. See Hansen (in preparation).

22. See, for example, Green (1998) and Martinson (1997).

23. Smith (1991, quotation is from p. 10).

24. Thorndike (1921, p. 378).

25. Thorndike (1921, p. 378).

26. Thorndike (1921, pp. 378-379).

27. Madaus and Raczek (1996).

28. Thorndike (1921, p. 379).

29. See, for example, Linn (1994).

30. Source: Collins (1997).

31. See National Education Goals Panel (1993, 1994, 1995).

32. For example, President Clinton promised in his 1997 State of the Union Address national tests in reading and math before the end of the decade.

33. For example, the trend in education legislation in the state of Indiana shows a dramatic rise in statues related to accountability and testing (Indiana Education Policy Center, 1994).

34. Pennsylvania rural middle school teacher, personal communication, February 11, 1998.

35. Michigan rural high school principal, personal communication, April 29, 1998.

36. Glaberson (1989).

37. See Stiggins and Conklin (1992).

38. The term authentic assessment was popularized by Wiggins (1989).

39. Tests consisting of selected response items, especially M-C items, are commonly described as objective tests. This is misleading because the selection and ordering of items and decisions as to which answers are correct (or more

correct than the other options) are subjective rather than objective. Likewise, machine scoring does not reduce subjectivity; it merely limits the number of persons who will provide subjective decisions as to which answers will be considered correct (Sutherland, 1996).

40. Among the early describers of portfolios were Archbald and Newmann (1988) and Paulson, Paulson, and Meyer (1991), who were the first strong proponents of the idea that students should be active developers and assessors of their own portfolios.

41. Adapted from displays of collections of measurements, profiles proliferated in Great Britain and Australia in the 1970s and 1980s (see Broadfoot, 1986; Broadfoot, James, McMeeking, Nuttall, & Stierer, 1988; Law, 1984).

42. Many examples of performance tasks are now available. Some early contemporary performance tasks were devised by Grant Wiggins at CLASS. Others have been developed by the New Standards Project, by the International Assessment of Educational Progress (IAEP), by the National Assessment of Educational Progress (NAEP), and by some states including Maryland and Connecticut.

43. See especially Raven (1992, pp. 85-87). Historical origins date to 1918 when progressive educator W. H. Kilpatrick began to promote "the project method," which ultimately "found itself a reasonably permanent place in schools throughout the world." A project was described as "an activity based on pupils' interests and undertaken by them with a firm purpose of broadening their experience and learning something seen by them to be worth the pursuit" (Connell, 1980, p. 283).

44. A summative evaluation is a final judgment of achievement, competence, or quality. A formative evaluation is ongoing, indicating progress to date and often suggesting improvements (see Scriven, 1990).

45. The best-known long-standing program involving demonstrations of mastery is to be found in Walden III High School's Rite of Passage Experience (R.O.P.E.) described in Archbald and Newman (1988), Mabry (1995c), and in Part 2 of the current text.

46. Margolis, De Champlain, and Klass (1998).

47. The paradigm is described in various writings about curriculum-based assessment but was first articulated in paradigmatic terms by Berlak (1992b).

48. Mabry (1995c). This approach to assessment is elaborated in Wiggins (1993).

49. Thorndike (1921, p. 378).

50. American Federation of Teachers, the National Council on Measurement in Education, and the National Education Association (1990).

51. The unfortunate state of teacher preparation opportunities summarized here is based on the author's experience in observing, reviewing, and evaluating professional development opportunities in a number of programs and a variety of texts intended for teachers as well as graduate courses in educational measurement (see, e.g., Mabry, 1996; see also Stiggins & Conklin, 1992).

Paradigms

A paradigm is a general conception, an understanding about what is true by which some practices are judged appropriate and others inappropriate.[1] The assessment paradigm under which we operate reveals what we believe it is possible and valuable to do in trying to understand what students have learned. Understanding different assessment paradigms can help us make careful choices about how we attempt to discover what students know and can do.

Three assessment paradigms can be found in the literature on educational measurement:

- Psychometric paradigm[2]
- Contextual paradigm[3]
- Personalized paradigm[4]

Each approach has strengths and weaknesses. Each is better for some purposes than for other purposes. Each has different implications for practice, even when the same type of assessment technique—such as portfolios—is used (see Table 2.1).

Too often, assessment reflects confusion, mismatching purposes to paradigms or techniques. Confusion in assessment policy typically produces systems that unintentionally limit the benefits of a given approach and that fail to accomplish fully the original assessment purposes. If we understand differences in assessment approaches, we are in a better position to develop coherent assessment systems and to coordinate assessment with teaching and learning.

TABLE 2.1 Assessment Paradigms

Psychometric	Contextual	Personalized
Standardized test content	Curriculum-sensitive test content	Student-sensitive test content
Standardized administration	Classroom settings common	Time and setting vary according to student
Objective items and formats	Both objective and subjective items	Subjective items, some student selection
Often machine scored	Teacher scored	Teacher or other scored
No self-evaluation	Self-evaluation important	Self-evaluation essential
Summative reporting and use of results	Formative use of results, may be summative	Formative use of results, may be summative

Psychometric Paradigm

In this century, as external measures have gradually overtaken pedagogic assessments as a basis for various educational decisions, the measurement of intelligence, aptitude, and achievement has taken a particular approach, which has been called the psychometric paradigm.[5] The primary method for this kind of measurement is the standardized multiple-choice test.

In the psychometric paradigm, the basic strategy for understanding student achievement is comparison. A student's performance is compared either to a predetermined standard or cut-score or to the performances of other test-takers. In a **norm-referenced test** (NRT), a student's performance is typically quantified as a score and compared with the scores of others presumed to be his or her peers.[6] To compare students' performances, test content, format, and administration is standardized. Comparison is facilitated when everyone must take the same test in the same way. Test questions or items are not selected for the purpose of maximizing students' opportunity to demonstrate what they know; test items are selected to maximize discrimination or differentiation among students. Scores are rank ordered. A student's achievement is determined by his or her rank, and often the rank is used to sort or select students for admission to special programs or special schools.

In a **criterion-referenced test** (CRT), a student's performance is compared to a predetermined criterion or standard. Criterion referencing gained popularity in the 1980s to avoid the problems of peer comparison experienced with NRTs. But criteria and standards tend to be set according to judgments of typical or satisfactory performance,[7] which blurs the distinction between CRTs and NRTs. In practice, CRTs tend to be heavily influenced by normative expectations or results—to be, in effect or to some extent, NRTs. That is, the cut-score that divides satisfactory from unsatisfactory performance is generally set on the basis of how students actually perform (or on predictions of how a minimally competent student would perform) than on judgments of what constitutes satisfactory performance. So student performances—not the judgments of content experts about what a student should be able to do to demonstrate minimum competence or mastery—are still compared to find the "norm," to set the cut-scores for each performance level. Criteria exist, but whether a test-taker has met the criteria is determined on the basis of how well other test-takers have performed.

In addition to the troubling competitiveness encouraged by norming and ranking, difficulties regarding test security, scoring, and reporting irregularities have been documented.[8] Still, standardized multiple-choice tests remain popular because of their aura of efficiency and objectivity. They can be quickly scanned and scored by machine, which supports a claim that they are efficient in time and money.[9] Also, machine scoring eliminates inconsistencies in human scoring, often worrisome when assessments are scored by two or more raters. And because many test items can be presented in a relatively short period of time, standardized multiple-choice tests are thought by many measurement experts to provide better content coverage than, by contrast, an essay test in which only one or a few questions can be answered in the same period of time.[10]

The psychometric paradigm has become so familiar it is commonly assumed to be the only approach to measuring intelligence or achievement, or the only valid or reliable or fair means of doing so. But even when they are technically flawless, legally justifiable, and highly predictive of some kinds of future performance, some say standardized tests are inadequate as educational assessments—judicially acceptable for selection purposes but not providing a good reflection of a student's unique achievement. Education failed to resist the assessments developed for differential psychology that rank and sort, as Robert Wood has argued:

> Education has always been vulnerable to psychometric incursions and influence. . . . Lacking a distinctive and self-confident view about the purpose of testing in schools and about what kinds of tests were suitable and unsuitable, [education] has, rather like a client state, looked on helplessly as psychometric doctrines and practices have been installed. . . . But education and differential psychology do not have the same aims.[11]

Taken as educational assessments, psychological assessments underrepresent the breadth, depth, detail, and particularity of students' real achievements, as noted by Robert Stake:

> Knowing the rank order of students as to proficiency is not at all the same as knowing what students know. . . . Education is not so much an achieving of some fixed standard. In a true sense, it requires unique and personal definition for each learner. . . . Education is a personal process and a personally unique accomplishment.[12]

The mismatch between the purposes of education and traditional means of assessing learning includes a mismatch between assessment and learning theory—not only constructivist learning theory but also theories of human and cognitive development.[13]

Moreover, in recent years, educators and educational researchers have recognized and documented serious human and educational consequences of standardized assessment of student achievement, such as

- narrowing of curricula to subjects, topics, and skills readily tested by multiple-choice items;[14]
- making curricula superficial and, in primary and preprimary grades, inappropriately academic;[15]
- reducing pedagogy to the teaching and memorizing of "miscellaneous dead facts";[16]
- diversion of funds and instructional time to testing and test preparation;[17]
- demoralization of students;[18]
- deprofessionalization of teachers;[19]
- misidentification of students—and misallocation of educational resources to them—because of test bias;[20]
- negative high-stakes consequences to students such as retention, placements in low academic tracks, and denial of graduation;[21]
- negative high-stakes consequences to teachers such as low evaluations, probation, and firing;[22]
- negative high-stakes consequences to schools such as public embarrassment, supervision, and loss of autonomy;[23]
- "score pollution" or raising scores without raising achievement;[24]
- reporting that is misleading about student achievement and about the quality of school programs[25] and that encourages inappropriate educational policy and practices;[26] and
- discouraging teachers and parents from remaining at and helping to improve low-scoring schools.[27]

It is becoming common to find claims that the tests' influence over education extends to the disempowerment of teachers as, increasingly, test developers determine what will be tested, which de facto determines what must be taught.[28] These matters are darkened by the commercial interests of test development corporations.[29]

Test developers reserve to themselves the authority to score and determine reporting formats. Machine scoring may be efficient, but it denies the practical expertise, the "knowing-in-action"[30] of teachers, suggesting they are incapable of evaluating their students' performances or achievement. While machine scoring helps to preserve the technical integrity of the test, it undermines the integrity of the human beings who administer and take it. Students are denied the opportunity to evaluate their own achievement and have little recourse or appeal if they feel scores misrepresent what they know.

For those who find unacceptable the image of the student as a passive sponge uncritically soaking up knowledge, the image of the test-taker whose brain is being wrung so that his or her knowledge might drip onto a bubble sheet is equally unappealing. A standardized test score, a single number based on a single performance under conditions many people find uncomfortable, may determine to a large or small extent a student's future educational opportunities, eventual employment, and life satisfaction. For this reason, Ralph Nader has called the Educational Testing Service, which produces many high-stakes tests,[31] the most powerful organization in the world.[32]

Contextual Paradigm

Teachers have not waited for measurement researchers and psychometricians[33] to develop an assessment paradigm appropriate for schools. The seriousness of the problems teachers experienced with standardized testing provoked changes in their own assessment practices, and these practices have encouraged a trend in large-scale testing toward performance assessment. Working on the basis of intuitive judgments about what kind of assessment was most appropriate for their students and their teaching, teachers led the way in the paradigm shift, their efforts predating and spurring state and national performance assessments. At present, performance assessment is mandated in 43 states.[34]

But intuitive judgments are difficult to articulate, and teachers and school administrators have lacked arguments as to why their new assessment practices are better, have lacked a rationale persuasive to test developers, policymakers, and the public. In 1992, Harold Berlak provided support to alternatives to standardized tests by offering a theoretical critique consistent with the empirical evidence against the tests. He argued against some traditional testing assumptions:

- that scores from the tests, which measure achievement only indirectly, may mean different, even contradictory, things to and about different people (i.e., the meaning of a test score is neither transparent nor universal);

- that the tests are *not* morally neutral but rather they exert a powerful influence over human decision making and relationships;

- that the tests may claim to measure only cognitive outcomes, but there can be no confident separation of cognitive, affective, and co-native[35] achievement; and
- that because the tests produce rankings but little information about what students know and can do, they are instruments not of feedback but of control and surveillance inconsistent with the principles of democracy and self-determination.

Amplified by his coauthors, Berlak offered instead a contextual paradigm in which

- assessments feature not standardized but curriculum-sensitive and authentic content (i.e., content that students have had a chance to learn and that might be useful in the world outside of school);
- testing is not limited to multiple-choice formats but may include constructed-response questions, problems, and tasks that are subjectively evaluated;
- students are tested in the natural, familiar settings of their own classrooms, where the context of learning matches the context of testing;
- teachers are empowered to use their professional judgments in evaluating students' efforts;
- students have opportunities to evaluate themselves; and
- assessment results not only inform teachers and others about what students have learned but also inform curriculum planning and the designing of future learning opportunities.

A primary distinction of the contextual paradigm is that the content of an assessment reflects the curricula students actually experience, not standardized content identical for every student regardless of their exposure to it. Contextualized assessments are designed to reveal what students have actually learned, not merely to rank and sort them. Where standardized tests produce the bottom-line comparisons often demanded by remote audiences (e.g., legislators, other policymakers, the public), feedback from curriculum-based assessments is useful to primary audiences (i.e., students, teachers, parents), supporting curriculum, rather than distorting it, and curriculum development and adaptation. The contextual paradigm honors teacher judgments and offers opportunity for students to demonstrate and to reflect on their complex knowledges and skills.

In an era of troubling disparities in allocation of educational funding and other resources,[36] contextualized assessment provides a needed opportunity for taking into account students' unequal learning opportunities. That is, even if educational resources are not fairly distributed, educational assessment need not reinforce that unfairness by using low scores to punish students who are already denied the best available learning opportunities. The discouraging record of resource allocation in the United States suggests that if equitable assessment depends on equitable school finance, we will never have equitable assessment.

There are problems with the contextual paradigm, too. Constructed-response items are time-consuming (and therefore expensive) to create and to score.[37] Because they are also time-consuming to administer, relatively few items can be offered in a test session, which limits coverage of the subject matter or domain tested and raises doubts about content validity.[38] Also, although there is no universal agreement about the appropriate purposes or content of education, some people do think there are certain things everyone should know,[39] things that might be neglected when assessment is aligned with many particular curricula rather than with common topics or skills.

Any scoring method is ultimately subjective, but scoring by human beings rather than by machines can result in distressing variability, as when one assessor awards a student a passing mark and another does not,[40] or when an assessor is subject to fatigue or other infringements on his or her judgment, which might cause variation in scores unrelated to the quality of students' performances.[41] Inconsistent scores are problems of reliability that are raising challenges and doubts regarding new assessment systems.[42]

Personalized Paradigm

A personalized approach to assessing student achievement better aligns with constructivist learning theory and individualized education because it assumes that

Everyone understands even the same things in different ways . . .	So tests should have personalized content.
Everyone has different interests and goals . . .	So tests should assess achievements that will reveal students' readiness to accomplish their own goals.
Everyone responds in different ways, for example, some are better at oral than at written expression . . .	So tests should allow students to perform in ways that afford them the best chance to show what they know.
Some people need more time to think things through (or need other differences in conditions) than others . . .	So tests should allow different conditions and amounts of time so test-takers can demonstrate what they know.

In a personalized paradigm implemented by some teachers,[43] content validity (the relevance and representativeness of test content to the domain tested[44]) is balanced with personal relevance (the relevance and representativeness of test content to the test-taker's learning, characteristics, and interests). By tailoring test content and administration and standards of quality for individuals, personalized assessment maximizes the opportunity to recognize and credit what students know rather than comparing their achievement to that of others or to prespecified standards.

In this approach, students may have much more input into and authority over their assessments. In some assessment programs, they may negotiate with teachers as to what test content is relevant to their individual achievements and what formats offer them the best opportunity for demonstrating knowledge and skills. Individuals often know best what they have learned and which examination formats offer them the best opportunity for demonstrating what they know. Students may help determine when and where tests should be taken. Results may be used to guide future work, to determine a summary indicator of achievement to date (e.g., a grade or score), or both.

In personalized assessment, personal or self-evaluation is crucial, more important than the evaluations of teachers and others because of the importance of self-knowledge as a basis for all understanding and the importance of metacognitive self-monitoring. Except within the personalized paradigm, no assessment is more neglected than self-assessment.

New assessment systems located entirely within the personalized paradigm tend to feature

Student-selected or student-teacher negotiated assessment content	"What can I do to demonstrate that my particular interest and work in this aspect of biology shows that I understand the subject?"
Student-selected or student-teacher negotiated assessment times and formats	"When will I be ready? How will I demonstrate what I've learned?"
Descriptive evaluations and justifications for them, rather than numerical scores, checklists, or rubrics	"This student's correct calculation of the sale price of carpeting for her bedroom showed she can apply her knowledge of area, percents, and decimals in practical situations."
Suggestions for correcting, improving, or extending student learning and other individualized feedback	"Although the student demonstrated understanding of the federal system of checks and balances, he should also be able to name state and local officials and explain how to cast a vote in his local precinct."

Student self-evaluation according to student-set or student-teacher negotiated criteria and standards	"I am pleased that my grammar has improved to the point where I am not embarrassed to let someone read this story, but I am disappointed that I didn't come up with a more realistic ending."

Assessment of individualized performances is a complex and ill-defined task. Flexibility regarding content, format, and setting requires unusual responsiveness by assessors. A machine could not score discourse assessment, for example, or handle the complexity of many performances, each customized for a particular student and judged by individualized standards constructed for and partly by the student. Human judgment, that of teachers and others, is necessary if assessment is to recognize the variety that human beings naturally exhibit.[45] Human beings constructing their own understandings—only personalized assessment fits with constructivism.

Because of the variability of products and processes assessed, prespecified criteria and standards are poor scoring guides for personalized assessment. They standardize assessment and draw attention away from the student's unique achievement. In the personalized paradigm, it is more appropriate for criteria and standards to be individualized, balancing considerations of quality with considerations of each student's background, opportunities, goals, and the like.

Individualized assessment tasks and individualized standards necessitate an entirely different type of training for assessors from that now typical. Currently, in large-scale performance assessment systems and in teacher workshops, raters and teachers are taught to apply standards or rubrics uniformly rather than to make judgments based on their understandings of content and measurement principles. Raters in large-scale performance assessment systems who award scores different from the scores awarded by their colleagues are retrained or dismissed.[46] That is, raters are expected to think and score identically, functioning almost as if they were a scoring machine.

Personalizing rather than standardizing assessment does not facilitate comparison of test-takers either to predetermined criteria or to other students. Rather than compare students to each other (i.e., normative assessment) or to one-size-fits-all standards (e.g., standards-based assessment, criterion-referenced assessment, mastery testing, minimum competency testing), personalized assessment features an **ipsative**[47] strategy in which teachers and others examine in detail an individual's accomplishments and shortcomings, his or her interests, progress over time, use of educational opportunities, and in-school and out-of-school engagements as a means of understanding as fully as possible what he or she has learned and can do.

Personalized assessment generates a much clearer and more detailed reflection of an individual's achievement[48] (see Figure 2.1) than does standardized assessment, which attends at least as much to such external referents as norms, standards, criteria, and rubrics as to the student and his or her actual achievement. Personalized assessment reflects the student's achievement with clarity and detail by flexibly adapting assessment to his or her skills and accomplishments so that teachers and parents and the student, too, can consider and understand what he or she knows and can do. It provides educationally useful information. Truly educational assessment, then, may be curriculum based (contextual paradigm) to see how well students have learned in class or individualized (personalized paradigm) to see what each student has learned within and without the curriculum.

But even those who want elaborate information about an individual student's achievements often also want external referents: How is this student doing in comparison to others his or her age (or in his or her grade or class)? Highlighting students' unique accomplishments and skills does not help much to answer this question. And many of the difficulties of the contextual paradigm are found or even exacerbated in the personalized paradigm: Scoring by human assessors again presents distressing variability, perhaps even more variability when students are assessed with different tasks and standards; assessments are even more time-consuming to create and to administer when both the tasks and the standards must be individualized; and coverage of a subject or of information everyone might be expected to master is even more questionable.

The difficulty of ensuring appropriate coverage of content was recognized in individualized education as early as 1928, when Dewey[49] and other supporters worried about progressive education's intellectual rigor and curricular comprehensiveness.[50] As noted with the contextualized assessment paradigm, similar concern has been expressed in recent times regarding performance assessment's attempt to cover content with a relatively small number of complex items, a problem intensified in individualized assessment. As curriculum-based assessment might neglect parts of the subject area not offered as part of the classroom learning opportunity, individualized assessment can also present a problem of content validity. We want to know what the test-taker knows about the subject area, not just what he or she knows about those questions that appear on the test; we want to generalize from the test to the domain. To infer what the student knows about the domain, the test needs to represent the domain. Because the time that can be reasonably allotted to testing is limited, choices about test content must be made. Are many, short multiple-choice questions preferable to a few, more time-consuming performance tasks? Will the student's learning be revealed better if the test attempts to measure the breadth of the entire subject matter or the depth of understanding in selected topics? If assessment involves not only complex but also personalized tasks, might content coverage be further compromised? Might rigor

Figure 2.1. Validity

    NOTE: Validity in assessment was illustrated as a rain puddle reflecting a child by teacher Lois Hedman of Vancouver, Washington, 1993. The clearer and more detailed the reflection in the puddle, the more valid the assessment. (Reprinted by permission of L. Hedman.)

suffer—might difficult topics be neglected if students are tested on what they found interesting enough to learn? It is not clear that these issues can be resolved to everyone's satisfaction, but perhaps a careful and conscious combination of strategies would serve better than the current overreliance on standardized assessments.

Because personalized assessment systems must be able to adapt to students and contexts, they present new challenges to practitioners. In a school or district or consortium, a personalized assessment system may require structuring agreements among teachers on basic principles and practices, frameworks for coherence that also have enough flexibility that teachers can fit assessment to their teaching styles, their subjects and grade levels, and their students' needs. A personalized assessment system cannot be static but must continuously adapt to the changing needs of students and classrooms. Structural coherence and dynamic and contextual flexibility are difficult to achieve simultaneously.

A Wave of Paradigm Shifts

Adopting the personalized paradigm requires radical assessment reform, reform that is occurring in some places[51] and that fits with other important educational changes:

- the shift in *learning theory* toward constructivism and developmental processes and away from behaviorism;

- the shift in *classroom roles*, seeing students as active and self-initiating learners rather than exhibiting passivity, and seeing teachers as facilitators and coaches rather than authoritative distributors of knowledge;

- the shift in *curriculum and pedagogy* toward inquiry, student responsibility, integration of knowledge, and cooperative and collaborative learning rather than direct instruction of compartmentalized subjects and facts;

- the shift in *school organization* toward site-based management, decentralization of authority, and empowerment and professionalization of teachers;

- the shift in *school choice* from schools with defined catchment areas to magnet, alternative, and choice schools that attract students with a variety of interests and learning styles;

- the shift in *educational research* toward qualitative understanding of complex, contextualized phenomena through integrated narratives rather than quantitative representation of isolated factors broadly generalized; and

- finally, gradually, perhaps, the shift in student *assessment* toward personalization and recognition of individual achievement rather than standardization in test-defined academic areas.

The underlying current propelling this wave of change is recognition of learning as a complex and profoundly individual phenomenon requiring enormous local flexibility and responsiveness. Decentralizing, the movement is toward first-level interest and responsibility, centering attention on individuals and small units rather than collectives, and toward acknowledging education as a variegated enterprise rather than a monolithic phenomenon that can be represented and evaluated on the basis of a few uniform factors for all schools. Against this movement is a contradictory undertow of centralization, which is apparent in large-scale assessment-based accountability systems,[52] development of state and national standards,[53] and widespread use of rubrics to operationalize standards for scoring new performance assessments.[54]

So trends in student assessment exhibit something like schizophrenia. Traditionalists and even some advocates of performance and alternative assessment demand that new measurement techniques be forced through the rusty old sieve of the psychometric paradigm, pressing especially for uniform "high standards for all" and standardization of assessments— even with techniques that facilitate individualization. Standards of achievement need not force standardization but, currently, most do.[55] In many new performance assessment systems, developers have unwittingly implemented new techniques within the old paradigm. The mismatch is apparent in systems that feature, for example,

- portfolios in which the contents are prescribed in advance, students and teachers having little option to select entries that would show a student's unique accomplishment;[56]

- performance tasks that prespecify what the student must do rather than discovering what he or she might think to do without prompting;[57]

- predetermined criteria, standards, or rubrics lacking any mechanism for crediting unique and unexpected aspects of performance;[58]

- reduction of feedback to a score or grade instead of detailed, individualized critique and suggestions;[59]

- normative strategies in which student performances are compared and perhaps ranked, rather than ipsative strategies in which a student's performance is judged according to the individual's strengths and weaknesses, opportunity to learn, interests, progress, and goals;

- rater training that demands that teachers think identically rather than exercising complex professional judgment;[60] and

- systems that do not offer the student a real opportunity for self-evaluation.

New assessment systems within the old paradigm inevitably show signs of internal conflict and self-limitation. For example, there is not much point in taking the time to create a portfolio or to devise, administer, and assess performance tasks that yield elaborate and highly individual information only to reduce evidence of achievement to a few scores. Some progress has been made in creating assessments that provide clearer reflections of students' accomplishments, but many of our new systems are the proverbial new wine in old skins.

The direction and sustainability of assessment change are not yet clear. Are today's first-generation alternative assessment practices a necessary first step gradually moving toward personalization, or are constructed-response items headed down the old road of standardization? Will one paradigm dominate, or will we learn to use paradigms selectively and purposefully? Will large-scale assessment take one course and classroom assessment another? Will alternative assessment be poorly implemented or too expensive? Will we become discouraged by the time and effort needed to create, administer, and score tasks and portfolios? Will we foist new and good assessment ideas on teachers who are unprepared, creating such chaos we yearn for the efficiency and orderliness of standardized multiple-choice tests? Will new assessment practices be overwhelmed by our appetite for comparable scores and simplistic bottom lines?

What is clear is that assessment has always exerted profound influence on the content and practice of education and that the effects of assessment ideology and policy are inevitably felt by students and teachers at the microlevel where teaching and learning occur.[61] Collectively, educators, parents, legislators and other policymakers, the public—*we* may fail to take the opportunity to reconsider what assessment should be and should do. But we have the best opportunity in this century to develop truly educational assessments of students as individuals and of what they have learned of the curricula their teachers and schools have provided—detailed reflections of each student's achievement.

Notes

1. For a discussion of paradigms and paradigm shifts, see Kuhn (1962). For a brief critique of Kuhn, see Scriven (1991, p. 253).

2. This term was used by Berlak (1992b) to refer to traditional standardized testing.

3. See Berlak (1992b).

4. See Mabry (1995c).

5. The term *psychometric*, from the Greek, means measurement of the mind. The term *psychometric paradigm* comes from Berlak (1992b).

6. In addition to the problem of selecting items to discriminate among test-takers rather than to examine what they have learned, an important problem is the presumption that the comparison group or norming sample is composed of peers. Scores from the population of students who make up the norming sample to which the performances of test-takers will later be compared are often several years old, sometimes predating important changes in theories, policy, and curricula; an example is the Wide Ranging Achievement Test 3 or WRAT3 (see Conoly & Impara, 1995, pp. 1108-1109). Sometimes, the norming sample took the test later in the year than actual test administration, giving the comparison group a greater opportunity to learn more information. Sometimes, norming samples come from those schools that happen to volunteer or that agree to be tested in exchange for financial compensation, circumstances that can render the norming group unrepresentative of the population of actual test-takers. Some standardized tests now use the group of test-takers as the norming sample, but there can be group variations from one year to the next which obstruct identification of trends.

7. See Impara and Plake (1997) and Kane (1994).

8. See, for example, Fisher and Smith (1991).

9. However, studies of the consumption of school resources devoted to test preparation challenge this claim (see Smith, 1991; see also U.S. General Accounting Office, 1993).

10. The content coverage of standardized tests has been challenged by studies showing that the tests neglect complex ideas and higher-order thinking (see Bowman & Peng, 1972) and that, rather than covering the curriculum, the curriculum is narrowed and distorted by being forced to cover the content of the tests (see Berliner & Biddle, 1995; Smith, 1991).

11. Wood (1990, p. 48).

12. Stake (1991, p. 7).

13. See Paris, Lawton, Turner, and Roth (1991) and Shepard (1991).

14. See Berliner and Biddle (1995), Smith (1991), and Wolf (1993).

15. Shepard and Smith (1988).

16. The quotation is from Meier (1983). Complaints that the tests prioritize facts over understanding date from the earliest days of standardized educational testing (Connell, 1980, p. 298). See also Bowman and Peng (1972) and Shepard and Dougherty (1991).

17. See Madaus and Raczek (1996), National Center for Fair and Open Testing (1994), and Smith (1991).

18. See Berliner and Biddle (1995) and Smith (1991).

19. See Berliner and Biddle (1995), Broadfoot (1996), Jaeger (1991), Nolen, Haladyna, and Haas (1992), and Smith (1991).

20. For example, gender bias (see Burton, 1996; Glaberson, 1989; Rosser, 1987), cultural bias (see Owen, 1985), socioeconomic bias (see College Board, 1990). See also Beckford and Cooley (1993), regarding a "racial gap" they decline to discuss as bias. Note that test developers refute claims of bias (see, e.g., Lightfoot-Clark, 1997).

21. See Brooks (1998a, 1998b).

22. For example, in the 1987 case of *St. Louis Teachers' Union v. St. Louis Board of Education*, teachers who had been placed on probation because of their students' low test scores sued for redress and won.

23. See Madaus (1991).

24. The term was first used by Haladyna, Nolen, and Haas (1991), who also discussed types of score pollution. See also Lichota (1981).

25. See Cannell (1987a, 1987b), Cooley and Bernauer (1991), Gray (1996), and Stake (1991).

26. See McAllister (1991), McLean (1996), Shepard and Smith (1988), and Stronach and Maclure (1996).

27. See McLaughlin (1991) and Wilson and Corbett (1989).

28. See Smith and Rottenberg (1991).

29. See Mabry and Daytner (1997) and Madaus and Raczek (1996).

30. Schön (1995).

31. In the 1980s, ETS became the contractor for administering the National Assessment of Educational Progress, planned by Ralph Tyler as a trend-monitoring survey (see Lapointe, 1986). In 1991, NAEP began to be used to compare performances by states.

32. Reported in "Sixty Years of Idiocy Is Enough" (1987).

33. The term is derived from Greek, meaning measurers of the mind.

34. Mabry, unpublished data. See Bond, Braskamp, van der Ploeg, and Roeber (1996) and Mabry and Daytner (1997).

35. The term *conative* refers to aspects of behavior involving determination, persistence, and volition, not appreciation and enjoyment, which are connoted by the term *affective* (see Raven, 1992).

36. See, for example, Darling-Hammond (1994) and Kozol (1992, 1995).

37. See, for example, O'Neil (1993) and U.S. General Accounting Office (1993).

38. See Burstein (1991), Frechtling (1991), and Hill and Hoover (1991). Content validity refers to whether the content of the test is fully relevant to and fully representative of the content of the domain or construct being tested (American Educational Research Association, American Psychological Association, & the National Council on Measurement in Education, 1985; Messick, 1989).

39. See, for example, Hirsch (1987) and GOALS 2000 (1994).

40. Reliability means consistency of scores (see Feldt & Brennan, 1989). When a student's performance is scored by two or more assessors, consistency among the scores is called interrater reliability. When two or more assessors disagree about the score for a performance, the scores are said to be unreliable.

41. Many difficulties related to the validity and reliability of assessments scored by human assessors are discussed in measurement textbooks such as Hopkins, Stanley, and Hopkins (1990).

42. For example, the Vermont portfolio system has been criticized as insufficiently reliable (Koretz, 1992, 1993; Koretz, Stecher, Klein, & McCaffrey, 1994).

43. After studying a teacher-developed assessment system at Walden III High School in Racine, Wisconsin (Mabry, 1992a, 1992b, 1995c), which assessed students' readiness to achieve their personal goals in life, I described the practices as a student-centered paradigm. A study of Pan Terra High School in Vancouver, Washington in 1997 (Mabry, in press-b) confirmed the usefulness of personalized student assessment. Individualized assessment has been described in the literature, especially by Grant Wiggins (1993).

44. The relevance and representativeness of test content to the domain tested is the primary guide to a test's content validity (Messick, 1989).

45. See Delandshere and Petrosky (1994).

46. See, for example, recommendations for protecting subjectively graded performance assessments from litigation in Phillips (1993). Another source is Craig Bensen, rater trained for scoring Oregon's state-mandated performance assessments (personal communication, July 1997).

47. In ipsative assessment, "scoring is useful in *intra*-individual comparison and not in *inter*-individual comparison" (Cohen, Montague, Nathanson, & Swerdlik, 1988, p. 312, emphasis in the original).

48. Clarity and detail of reflection are related to the important issue of validity in Chapter 4.

49. Connell (1980, p. 287).

50. Rugg and Schumaker (1928).

51. In addition to the assessment systems mentioned earlier at Walden and Pan Terra High Schools, exploration of personalized assessment is occurring in Chicago by the Lake View Education and Arts Partnership (LEAP), described in Chapter 7 of this volume.

52. In 1994, 47 states had testing programs, and 31 states reported large-scale performance assessments were part of their testing programs (Bond, 1994; Mabry & Daytner, 1997). As of this writing, 43 states report use of performance assessments (Mabry, unpublished data).

53. See, for example, National Education Goals Panel (1993, 1994, 1995). At the state level, in 1997, 44 states reported they were revising their standards and 5 others reported they were developing standards—all but Iowa (Collins, 1997; see also Massell, Kirst, & Hoppe, 1997).

54. In 1994-1995, in 27 states, use of some kind of analytic scoring guide, often a rubric, was reported (Mabry & Daytner, 1997), and many new assessment materials and workshops stress development and use of rubrics (see Burke, 1994, for an example of such materials, and Mabry, 1996, for an evaluation of assessment training using such materials). Currently, 34 states use writing rubrics (Mabry, 1999).

55. For an example of standards that do not press standardization, see National Council of Teachers of Mathematics (1989). See also Wiggins (1991), for a discussion of standards without standardization.

56. See Vermont Department of Education (1991).

57. For example, not fully crediting correct answers that fail to use an expected strategy.

58. See, for example, state writing rubrics from Vermont (Vermont Department of Education, 1991) and Kentucky (Kentucky Department of Education, 1994). See also Mabry (1999).

59. The validity of numerical representation of complex performances has been questioned by Delandshere and Petrosky (1998).

60. C. Bensen, personal communication, July 1997, and Colvin (1997).

61. For a theoretical model of the interconnectedness of ideology, policy, and practice, see Bronfenbrenner (1979).

CHAPTER
THREE

Purposes

Measurement textbooks typically state that testing supports education by clarifying objectives, providing feedback to teachers and students, motivating and even facilitating learning, and enhancing quality control. Different kinds of tests are classified as appropriate for specific purposes such as diagnosing poor achievement, making placement decisions, certifying mastery, and evaluating programs and instruction.[1]

This is an idealized view. Teachers have seldom found claims of the usefulness of standardized multiple-choice achievement tests to be warranted.[2] Some claims exaggerate what these tests do (e.g., provide feedback[3]); some claims seem oddly out of sequence (e.g., clarify objectives as an assessment process rather than as a curriculum development process[4]); some claims seem inconsistent with actual experience (e.g., some would say the tests raise anxiety more than they motivate learning, and some would say educational quality has been hurt more than helped by the tests).

Some test purposes might be achieved in other, perhaps better, ways or through nontraditional approaches to assessment. For example, to address quality control through accountability, one option almost never seriously considered is the choice between

- documenting student performance, and
- assessing student performance.

All the new assessment techniques noted earlier—portfolios, profiles, performance tasks, projects, demonstrations of mastery, discourse assessment, and simulations—may be used to generate evidence of student learning. Portfolios and other techniques that yield tangible products provide documentation of student achievement. That these products can be assessed does not mean that they must be. Evidence of achievement in a portfolio, for instance, can stand as a record of what a student has learned whether or not the portfolio is formally evaluated or awarded a score or grade.[5] Similarly, school accountability does not require student assessment, although this is now our chief strategy, but may be accomplished by documentation of student learning within programs and openness to inspection.[6] With new as well as traditional methods of student assessment, we should consider some fundamental questions, not only how but also whether and when to assess evidence of student learning.

Matching Purpose to Strategy

What do we want to assess—and do we really need to assess it? Why do we want to assess it—what will we do with the results? How should we assess—how can we get the kind of information we need? These questions and one other—How can we assess without harmful side effects?—are important considerations. Different answers suggest vastly different assessment programs. Simply allowing assessment to happen without attention to purpose, without sensitive matching of assessment strategy to information needs and contexts, can result in frustration, time-consuming effort without the desired recompense. Falling back on old test habits, rather than questioning their efficacy for current aims, may even prove counterproductive.

What do we want to assess? There are educational tests intended to measure intelligence, aptitude, achievement—more accurately, they provide data on the basis of which we infer intelligence, aptitude, or achievement. Although the names of standardized tests suggest that one or another of these aspects of human functioning can be isolated and measured, they are not practically separable. There are also psychological tests of such aspects as latent traits and attitudes, and these aspects may also play a role in the results. Trying to measure achievement alone and to exclude other aspects[7] is not possible. An additional complication is that achievement per se is an extremely broad measurement target, too broad for any single assessment.

What will we do with the results? How can we get the kind of information we need? When we have some particular type of achievement in focus—say, biology or long division—assessment may still serve different purposes that suggest different strategies. For example, many tests of educational achievement are designed to report individual student learning. Different kinds of standardized achievement tests indicate a student's achievement in different ways: relative to other test-takers or relative to a criterion or standard or cut-score.[8] If we want to use test scores to select or place students in particular programs or schools, we may want to admit everyone who has met a particular criterion, so we may want achievement information relative to a criterion or standard or cut-score. Criterion-referenced or standards-based tests should tell whether applicants have requisite knowledge and skills, so these tests should be composed of items that test for this. Or we may want to admit only the top 10% of applicants, or to fill 20 vacancies with the top performers among the applicants, so we may want achievement information that ranks test-takers. Tests that rank test-takers are composed of items that maximize distinctions among performances to facilitate rankings.

Some tests are intended not to report individual results but to indicate the performance of a group, program, or institution, to monitor trends across time. For example, from 1969, the National Assessment of Educational Progress (NAEP), mandated by Congress in response to political concerns more than in answer to questions of educational policy, has functioned as a survey to monitor trends in the nation's educational achievement. Its role is changing—NAEP was revised beginning in 1991 to compare state achievement levels[9]—and, now, the developing national assessments are "essentially part of NAEP."[10] For monitoring trends, it is not necessary for every student to take the NAEP tests (a test administration procedure referred to as **full census testing**); rather, a sample of test-takers representative of students across the country are tested, each on parts of the test rather than on the entire test[11] (a test administration procedure referred to as **matrix sampling**). Because no student takes the full test in matrix sampling, individual student scores do not exist and cannot be aggregated or compared, keeping the emphasis on national rather than individual student issues.

How can we assess without harmful side effects? Tests intended to measure the achievement of individuals are not typically suitable for measuring program quality as well. Although the program evaluation community characteristically warns against aggregation of individual scores as a basis for judging the quality of educational programs,[12] this is frequently done. Test developers do not take responsibility for unintended, unvalidated uses of test scores. Their warnings appear unhighlighted in test documentation, easily neglected by immediate users, sometimes school people relatively unsophisticated in such matters. This unbalanced attribution of responsibility to immediate users regarding unvalidated test use is apparent in the introduction and in two standards currently proposed for the upcoming revision of the *Standards for Educational and Psychological Testing:*

It is difficult to assign precise responsibility for addressing various standards to specific participants in the testing process. This document begins with a series of chapters on the test development process, which focus primarily on the responsibilities of test developers, and then turns to specific uses and applications, which focus primarily on responsibilities of test users.[13]

Standard 1.3 If validity for some common or likely interpretation has not been investigated, or is inconsistent with available evidence, that fact should be made clear, and potential users should be cautioned about making unsupported interpretations.

Standard 1.4 If a test is used in a way other than those recommended, it is incumbent on the user to justify the new use, collecting new evidence if necessary.[14]

Admittedly, test developers cannot practically control for all uses of their tests, but the history of testing practice suggests it is equally impractical for test users to be expected to understand this admonition or to collect validity evidence to support their particular uses. It is unlikely that validity will be well protected by such standards. For example, consider the conclusion from a review of changes in the use of test scores in the admissions policies of seven colleges and universities including Harvard and Johns Hopkins:

Schools often use standardized tests unquestioningly. In determining the utility of the tests, they rely on the conclusions of studies conducted by the test publishers or organizations that derive much of their income from student test fees. But these institutions have an obvious interest in legitimizing and perpetuating testing. We cannot assume that their studies are impartial. Universities have little motivation to examine the tests themselves because they are not charged for their use of the tests.[15]

Such uncritical use even by prestigious institutions is unfortunate because education has been badly harmed by misuse of tests and test scores. Good teachers and programs for low-performing students have been jeopardized by low scores on tests that were not designed to measure instructional effectiveness or program quality. Students have been denied admittance to schools and programs. It is a travesty that educators who are victimized by the tests are made to bear responsibility for validating them, a responsibility for which few are trained.

One significant problem could be avoided by reserving full census testing for purposes of reporting individuals' achievement and matrix sampling for purposes of evaluating programs and monitoring trends. This would curb the score pollution found in tests of individual student achievement by removing the incentive to inflate these scores from those who administer tests and who also have a vested interest in the programs that might be judged on the basis of aggregated individual scores.

Diagnostic testing. Often, we want assessments that do more than indicate achievement levels: We want tests that specify difficulties so that remediation can be pinpointed and curricula revised. We have tests that claim to diagnose conceptual errors and faulty skills, but tests that provide only scores and tests that merely rank test-takers offer little information of this kind. The educational utility of these tests is low because scores and rankings do not identify weaknesses in either student performance or educational delivery,[16] although laypersons often presume that a purpose of such tests is to provide such information. Some doubt the diagnostic capacity of tests generally.

The item selection as well as the detail in reporting results of diagnostic tests differs from that of tests that simply indicate achievement levels or rankings. Items in diagnostic tests are not chosen to discriminate among test-takers or to assign performance levels but rather to identify whether test-takers are proficient regarding certain information and processes and whether they suffer from certain misconceptions. Diagnostic tests may be no less standardized than standards-based or placement tests, but the purpose dictates different content and reporting.

Authenticity

If we want to find out whether test-takers can function well outside the school setting, we are likely to want **authentic assessments.** The distinguishing characteristic here is similarity or fidelity to important tasks beyond those of the classroom. Assessments that would not have meaning in nonschool settings, such as a vocabulary test or a test of historical dates, are distinguished from authentic assessments, such as writing a letter or discussing the influence of antitrust laws on conditions for workers. In life, we do not take vocabulary tests, but we do write letters that require use of vocabulary. In life, we are rarely required to recall historical dates, but it behooves us to understand how one event influences another or how a law affects working and living conditions, and we talk about such things.

Authenticity is a matter of degree, some tasks and some performances more authentic or lifelike than others. Some cognitively useful activities better lend themselves to real or realistic demonstration of skills than others. For example, the engagement of foreign language students in conversation in French is more authentic than is providing them with grammar worksheets, although they are likely to benefit from activities that teach and evaluate their understanding of linguistic structure. As attention to many topics and skills is beneficial for students, recourse to a variety of teaching and assessment methods and opportunities is also helpful, especially when their use is informed, thoughtful, and well targeted.

Authentic assessment may be particularly important in some areas. For example, medical education has increasingly moved to authentic assessments to assure that students can perform well in clinical situations, not just on paper-and-pencil tests. For example, medical students' skills in taking patient histories and diagnosing medical conditions are now tested using standardized patients, persons trained to simulate illnesses as if they were seeking treatment and to evaluate the skills demonstrated by medical students.

Feasibility and Utility

In attending to assessment purposes, a choice between assessment paradigms or strategies may involve trading off advantages and disadvantages. Advantages in educational utility sometimes entail disadvantages in feasibility. For example:

Psychometric paradigm	*Advantages*	*Disadvantages*
Standardized assessment	Efficient	Negative student effects
	Public credibility	Negative school effects
	Well-developed and institutionalized technology	Limited utility for curriculum planning or remediation
	Tells relative position or rank or achievement relative to a standard or criterion	Gives little detail about what students know and can do

Whether norm referenced, criterion referenced, or standards based, the feasibility of standardized testing as the prime strategy of the psychometric paradigm is aided by the efficiency of machine scoring and established systems of distribution, administration, and dissemination of results and by public acceptance of the method. But some of these feasibility pluses actually inhibit the educational usefulness of standardized testing: Machine scoring is efficient, but it deprofessionalizes teachers; providing only information about ranking or about performance levels reduces the information processing load, but it severely inhibits the usefulness of information gained, offering little specific information about how to teach or reteach.

Some standards-based performance assessments offer more instructionally useful information, but this is usually limited to brief information regarding performance related to prespecified criteria. The low utility of this type of information was reported by school personnel in Michigan, for example, discussing that state's standards-based 1998 High School Proficiency Test. A principal stated that his high school tried to make curricular improvements in response to test results each year but was stymied by lack of feedback regarding the state's expectations and specific data regarding student performance. Of the writing component of the test, he reported,

> We do a good job teaching writing, and we write across the curriculum. We have a lot of good writers but, last year, some of them got novice [one of the performance levels] in writing. With some, we applied to have their papers rescored, and they came back the same. It's something of a mystery.[17]

Although the scoring criteria were described in the test administration booklet and were known to the school's attentive personnel, a high school teacher at the same school expressed similar desire for unavailable performance information:

> Even kids who've gotten As in my composition classes—and I'm a very tough teacher, a very tough grader—got awful scores. The number of students who were classified as nonproficient on the test was horrendous. Many of these kids had straight As. I don't know what the criteria are. Even our salutatorian was scored as nonproficient. I don't get it. So, I'm not sure what they're looking for.[18]

Equally damning from an educational point of view, this teacher found the criteria on which feedback was available to be superficial, unimportant, and instructionally irrelevant:

> The criteria are not things I'd pick out for teaching. They don't focus on quality—not criteria like "flow." That's fixable. A piece of writing can be a little bit choppy and still be good. Sometimes I get the impression the rubrics were written by people who haven't been in a high school English classroom since Moses was a baby. They don't know what quality is in a student paper. It's bizarre.[19]

The curriculum sensitivity featured in the contextualized assessment paradigm also comes at a cost:

Contextual paradigm	Advantages	Disadvantages
Curriculum-based assessment	Informs instruction	May parochialize curricula
	Empowers teachers	Teachers untrained in measurement make errors
	Tells how well students learned what was intended	Does not tell how students performed in comparison to others in other places

The educational utility of curriculum-based tests, in contrast to curriculum-insensitive standardized tests, is stronger, but general reference points are lost when information is limited to the classroom curriculum, the conditions, and the students at hand. For educators, this is often a good trade, but policymakers and a public hungry for simple comparisons are unlikely to agree.

Personalization pushes the benefits farther and exacerbates the costs:

Personalized paradigm	*Advantages*	*Disadvantages*
Individualized assessment	Informs sensitive instruction	Strong demands on judgment and flexibility
	Empowers students	Assessors untrained in measurement make errors
	Empowers teachers	Little information as to how students performed in comparison to curriculum or to others
	Details what students know and can do	

Despite the clear benefit personalization offers for adapting education to individuals as implicitly prescribed by constructivist learning theory, the intellectual and resource demands of developing individualized standards and responding to a wide variety of performance types are daunting. Personalized assessment has been well established in some small-scale, school-based systems.[20] But personalization's demand for familiarity with and sustained attention to individuals raises the issue of feasibility for large-scale implementation: When there are many test-takers or applicants, is it possible to focus on individuals? Portfolios were established on a districtwide scale in Pittsburgh in the late 1980s and early 1990s where, after five years, the district director of research, evaluation, and test development, Paul LeMahieu, reported, "The simple fact [is] that it worked, [so] it's safe to say, 'Yes, it can work.' If it can work this well in a situation where money is as tight as here, I don't see how it can't work."[21]

Notes

1. See, for example, Hopkins, Stanley, and Hopkins (1990, pp. 11-16) and Gronlund (1993, pp. 2-8).

2. See Stiggins and Conklin (1992).

3. Especially feedback teachers and students would find useful as in the sense described by Wiggins (1993). Feedback from tests and from other assessments can be misleading because of problems in representing and discerning

meaning in scores or grades. One student's 80th percentile score does not represent the same achievement as another student's; an A from one teacher does not mean the same thing as an A from another.

4. Although it is sometimes advised that curriculum be planned backwards, beginning with assessment (see Wiggins, 1998), this may have constraining effects on education. As to which should be prior, a related finding regarding curriculum and assessment personnel by LeMahieu and Eresh (1996) asserts, based on the Arts PROPEL portfolio experience in Pittsburgh, that giving priority to assessment staff over curriculum staff "is not likely" to result in "high quality curricular and instructional improvements" (pp. 139-140).

5. At this point, it may be useful to consider traditional distinctions: (1) assessment, "a process by which things are differentiated . . . not limited to the use of highly developed and refined instruments" (Hopkins et al., 1990, p. 1); (2) evaluation, "determining the worth or merit of an evaluation object (whatever is evaluated)" (Worthen, Sanders, & Fitzpatrick, 1997, p. 5); and (3) measurement, "any differentiation among members of a class of things that is expressed numerically" (Hopkins et al., 1990, p. 1).

6. See House (1996) for an argument that openness to public scrutiny is preferable to testing as a means of accountability.

7. These aspects are referred to as constructs (see Chapter 4; also Cronbach & Meehl, 1955).

8. These approaches are discussed in greater detail when scoring differences are presented in Chapter 4.

9. See Haertel and Mullis (1996).

10. Lawton (1997).

11. Viadero (1997).

12. Program evaluators' move away from use of test scores as important indicators of educational quality has been well documented (see, e.g., Madaus, Scriven, & Stufflebeam, 1987; Worthen, Sanders, & Fitzpatrick, 1997). This is because achievement levels reflect not only the quality of educational programming but also such determiners as available funding and socioeconomic status, which can overwhelm program quality in test scores.

13. American Educational Research Association, American Psychological Association, and the National Council on Measurement in Education (AERA, APA, NCME; 1998, Introduction, p. 2).

14. AERA, APA, NCME (1998, Chapter 1, p. 15).

15. Allina (1991, p. 10). Also reported in the *Boston Globe*, November 7, 1987, and the *Chronicle of Higher Education*, November 11, 1987.

16. Mabry, Daytner, and Aldarondo (1999) and Stiggins and Conklin (1992).

17. Anonymous Michigan principal, personal communication, April 29, 1998.

18. Anonymous Michigan teacher, personal communication, April 29, 1998.

19. Anonymous Michigan teacher, personal communication, April 29, 1998.

20. Examples of personalized assessment can be found in the Rite of Passage Experience at Walden III High School in Racine, Wisconsin (Mabry, 1995c) and at Pan Terra High School in Vancouver, Washington (Mabry, in preparation-b).

21. Rothman (1992).

FOUR

Scoring

Consciously or unconsciously, developers of assessment systems make some basic decisions. Awareness of terms and principles helps to ensure coherence, avoid conflict within an assessment system, and facilitate the development of a rationale for the system. Some fundamental decisions concern the manner in which student performances will be scored. As noted, three distinctive strategies are apparent in current assessment systems:

Normative scoring: Comparing students' performances to those of others, formally or informally ranking them, and awarding high scores to those with top performances and low scores to those with low performances even if everyone performed well or no one did

Examples: (1) percentiles, stanines, and other standard scores that rank a student's score against the scores of a norming sample or test group; (2) grading on a curve; and (3) any grading based on intuitive rankings more than on actual quality of performance

Criterion-referenced or standards-based scoring: Comparing students' performances to criteria or standards, perhaps ranking them, and awarding high scores to those whose performances meet or exceed criteria or standards and low scores to those whose performances do not

Examples: (1) standards-based assessment, (2) criterion-referenced testing, (3) mastery testing, and (4) minimum-competency testing

Ipsative scoring: Not comparing a student's performance to an external referent but, rather, judging quality and competence on the basis of personal strengths and weaknesses, skills, progress over time, opportunity to learn, interests, goals, academic and personal background, and other factors that affect performance

Examples: (1) documenting the learning of special education students using individualized education plans (IEPs); (2) in creative arts, judging original products and unique skills, as in painting and drama; and (3) evaluating student work without reference to standards, preordinate criteria, rubrics, or other students

Normative Assessment

The assumption of normalcy is that scores (or other numerical indicators), when plotted on a scale, will cluster around a midpoint and that, the farther from the center, the fewer scores will be found. In nature, where many phenomena can be unambiguously measured, such as height and weight, this central tendency is often observed. Unsurprisingly, an early use of the normal curve or bell-shaped curve[1] was in the study of agriculture. But for those human characteristics that must be inferred, such as intelligence or aptitude or scholastic achievement, there is no natural yardstick. The numbers assigned to the measures of features and the scales on which those numbers are plotted are arbitrary, and the grounds for claiming normalcy open to question. Normalcy is often claimed. Less often is it acknowledged that we may find what we are looking for because we are looking for it and that measures designed to anticipate normalcy are likely to produce results described as normal curves.

As noted, in normative assessment, a student's achievement is determined by comparison to others, either the rest of the test-takers or a sample, a comparison group. The normative assumption that students' achievement can be described by a normal curve, with a few students attaining very high and very low scores but most scoring in the midrange, is problematic in educational assessment for several reasons. First, it is not clear that achievement does or should exhibit central tendency. Frequent claims that all students can learn and that all students should master certain content suggests that most students should attain high scores. Some teachers do not think it is normal for only a few students to earn the highest scores; they think it is a signal that reteaching is needed, perhaps using different instructional methods or materials.

But test developers take a different view. Norm-referenced tests assume normalcy, that the distribution of scores on achievement tests will be described by a normal curve. Developers construct such tests more to differentiate among test-takers than to test what each has actually achieved. For instance, items that many are likely to know—that will reveal that nearly everyone has learned these bits of information—are few, disdained in favor of items that will distinguish better between high scorers and low scorers, a measure of discrimination more than of achievement likely to result in an overall distribution of scores that follow the normal curve. Then they convert actual scores, raw scores, to standard scores by assigning them to points on a graph in accordance with the normal curve. Such processes assume normalcy and do result in normal curve distributions—but is this because achievement is normally distributed? Or because the assumption of normalcy led to the development of a testing technology aligned with the assumption that, not at all coincidentally, tends to prove the assumption? If the latter, test developers' claims of the quality of their tests are undermined by the possibility that all who did well on the test may not have received a high score and vice versa.

Second, normative assessment pits students against each other in a forced competition that is counter-educational because it discourages students from learning from each other and developing team competencies. Third, standard scores from norm-referenced tests are, by nature, rankings, half of which will declare that students are below the average, a visible humiliation. Most students want to do much better than average, and most parents want this, too. Calculating standard scores by comparing each student's performance to the average[2] ensures that many will be disappointed. Some students become discouraged and test phobic.

Although it is useful to know how a student has performed in reference to peers, a student's rank actually conveys relatively little information about what the student has learned, a problem exacerbated by test security, denial of opportunity to see the items that were missed. Norm-referenced tests are not intended to provide detailed information about student knowledge and skills, and they do not.

Criterion-Referenced Assessment

Criterion-referenced assessment is an evaluation based on criteria and/or standards. In scoring student achievement, criteria tell what the student must do. As an example, the criteria listed in Table 4.1 are from the writing portfolio system developed in Vermont at the beginning of this decade. At the state's direction, participating Vermont schools were to include in fourth- and eighth-grade students' portfolios:

- a table of contents;
- a writing chosen as the student's "best piece";
- a letter from the student about the "best piece";
- a creative writing such as a poem, story, or play;
- a "personal response" to an outing such as a trip to a museum, play, or sports event; and
- a prose writing from a subject area other than English/language arts (three prose pieces for eighth graders).[3]

TABLE 4.1 Criteria From the Vermont Writing Portfolio System

Purpose	Organization	Details	Voice/Tone	Usage/Mechanics/Grammar

SOURCE: Vermont Department of Education (1991). The rubric was used until 1998.

These criteria state which writing features will be scored. For example, a student writer will be credited for good organization but not for persuasiveness.

Standards tell how well students must perform relative to the criteria. Performance standards are typically embodied in measurement scales, for example, standards for the Vermont writing portfolios are stated as a 4-point scale: *extensively, frequently, sometimes,* and *rarely.* Vermont did not list numbers on its Analytic Assessment Guide, but many measurement scales do include numbers, letters, or other indicators. Measurement scales are in common use in schools. For example, letter grades are a 5-point measurement scale, with an A being the high point on the scale and an F being the low point. Or letter grades can involve a 15-point measurement scale from A+ to F–. In primary grades, in some subjects, and for some assignments, teachers use 3-point measurement scales: E for *excellent,* S for *satisfactory,* and N for *needs improvement* or +, ✓, and –, respectively. Pass-fail courses use a 2-point measurement scale.

Rubrics

Put together, criteria and standards create one common type of rubric. Vermont's Analytic Assessment Guide was a rubric for scoring writing portfolios, a chart that listed criteria horizontally and standards vertically (see Table 4.2). Measurement standards, scales, and rubrics are often anchored with descriptors (see Table 4.3).

Rubrics can be subject specific. For example, the Vermont writing rubric was used to score all writing—in any genre, in response to any prompt or assignment, in any of the grade levels assessed—for the state portfolios. Alternatively, rubrics can be specific to a unit, a lesson, or a task.

For example, the rubric shown in Table 4.4 was constructed for the purpose of assessing an instructional unit that combined study of the Bill of Rights with study of textile arts, a unit developed by Chicago teacher Lourdes Silva and visual artist Abbey Gonzales. The bilingual seventh- and eighth-grade students, all of whom had limited English proficiency and many of whom were recent immigrants from Mexico and South and Central America, studied not only the provisions of the Bill of Rights but also the historical and contemporary contexts of the document and its differential impact of identifiable groups, including themselves and their

TABLE 4.2 Criteria and Standards From Vermont's Analytic Assessment Guide for Writing Portfolios

Criteria

Standards	Purpose	Organi-zation	Details	Voice/Tone	Usage/Mechanics/Grammar
Extensively					
Frequently					
Sometimes					
Rarely					

SOURCE: Vermont Department of Education (1991).

TABLE 4.3 Vermont's Analytic Assessment Guide for Writing Portfolios, Showing Abbreviated Anchors

Purpose	*Organization*	*Details*	*Voice/Tone*	*Usage/Mechanics/Grammar*
Extensively: Establishes and maintains a clear purpose . . .	Extensively: Organized from beginning to end . . .	Extensively: Details are effective, vivid, explicit, and/or pertinent	Extensively: Distinctive voice evident . . .	Extensively: Few, if any, errors are evident relative to length and complexity
Frequently: Establishes a purpose . . .	Frequently: Organized but may have minor lapses in unity or coherence . . .	Frequently: Details are elaborated and appropriate	Frequently: Evidence of voice . . .	Frequently: Some errors are present
Sometimes: Attempts to establish a purpose . . .	Sometimes: Inconsistencies in unity and/or coherence . . .	Sometimes: Details lack elaboration or are repetitious	Sometimes: Evidence of beginning sense of voice . . .	Sometimes: Multiple errors and/or patterns of errors are evident
Rarely: Does not estab-lish a clear purpose . . .	Rarely: Serious errors in organization . . .	Rarely: Details are ran-dom, inappro-priate, or barely apparent	Rarely: Little or no voice evident . . .	Rarely: Errors are fre-quent and severe

SOURCE: Vermont Department of Education (1991).

TABLE 4.4 Rubric for Assessing a Lake View Education and Arts Partnership (LEAP) Unit Combining Social Studies and Fabric Arts

Bill of Rights Quilt, Assessment for _____
(student's name)

Subjects or Categories	Aspects to Assess	Narrative Assessments and Who Will Assess
History	Understanding of Bill of Rights	Teacher's assessment:
History	Understanding of original political context of Bill of Rights	Student self-evaluation: Teacher's assessment:
History	Understanding of current political context of Bill of Rights	Teacher's assessment: Classmate's comments/assessment:
Personal	Relating Bill of Rights to self	Student self-evaluation:
Art	Originality	Teacher's assessment:
Art	Self-expression	Student self-evaluation:
Art	Craftsmanship	Teacher's assessment: Classmate's comments/assessment:
Oral language	Increased English vocabulary	Teacher's assessment: Other teachers' assessments:
Oral language	Increased fluency of expression in English	Teacher's assessment: Other teachers' assessments:
Group skills	Leadership	Student self-evaluation: Teacher's assessment: Teammate's comments/assessment:
Group skills	Conflict resolution	Student self-evaluation: Teacher's assessment:
Other (specify)		

own families. One of the ways students expressed what they had learned was in the creation of a quilt, in which each of the squares creatively illustrated student understanding of one or more of the ten provisions. The choice of textile arts for the unit's integration of academics and the arts was based on the importance of textiles in the cultures of the students' families.

ABLE 4.5 A Blank Rubric: Performance Aspects to Assess and Assessors

Subjects or Categories	Aspects to Assess	Narrative Assessments and Who Will Assess
Other		

In this unit, student achievement was to be assessed in several areas: social studies knowledge and critical thinking, artistic skills and aesthetics, language proficiency, and teamwork. The rubric for this unit needed to be attentive to these different areas of achievement. Moreover, the instructors' wish for the unit to contribute to students' development of personal understandings suggested the usefulness of self-evaluation, and the development of team skills suggested the usefulness of peer evaluation. The rubric in Table 4.4 is a one-page abbreviation of the one developed for this unit, the original of which had more categories and more space for evaluative comments by different assessors.

The blank rubric in Table 4.5 is one that could be adapted for other units. This blank rubric can be filled in (second column) with the planned objectives. Care must be taken so that all objectives are not treated as equally important, if they are not, and so that an accumulation of scores on several low-level objectives do not overwhelm scores on a few highly important objectives. An *Other* column adds important flexibility, allowing the assessor to credit students for accomplishments that were unanticipated at the start. This example shows how the chart could be used to keep track of each student's assessments, one chart per student. Note that more room would be needed for assessor's comments.

Explicit or Implicit Scoring Criteria

Rubrics are explicit statements of scoring criteria and performance standards. Criteria and standards are either

- **explicit,** when written statements or descriptors, rubrics, checklists, or other guides are used in determining grades, scores, or evaluations of the quality of student performances; or
- **implicit,** when teachers and other assessors evaluate the quality of student performances on the basis of their observations and professional experience and expertise without reference to formal guidelines.

It has become a common presumption that explicit criteria are necessary for good or reliable measurement.[4] This presumption should be critically examined. Explicit criteria fit with the psychometric paradigm. There, tests are typically developed by stating in advance what all students should know (i.e., should be tested on), by creating test questions on predetermined topics and difficulty levels, and often by drawing from a pool of field-tested items to construct the test as a whole. By contrast, new forms of assessment require students to construct responses rather than selecting from among predetermined options. Students will give many different answers, some creative or unexpected. The variations in their responses suggest that prespecified, explicit criteria may not be useful in scoring answers. An example is the following story of the barometer problem.

The Barometer Problem[5]

A physics instructor offered the following question on an examination:

Show how it is possible to determine the height of a tall building with the aid of a barometer.

A student responded with this answer:

Take the barometer to the top of the building, attach a long rope to it, lower the barometer to the street, and then bring it up, measuring the length of the rope. The length of the rope is the height of the building.

Interesting, but should the student get credit? The instructor intended to award no credit but, asked to referee, I pointed out the student had a strong case for full credit, having answered correctly. But full credit could contribute to an invalid inference the student knew some physics, which the answer did not confirm. It was agreed the student would have a second chance, and I would act as proctor.

As agreed, I gave the student six minutes to answer, warning him the answer should show some knowledge of physics. After five minutes, he had written nothing. I asked if he wished to give up, but he said he had many answers and was thinking which was the best. In the next minute, he dashed off his answer:

> Take the barometer to the top of the building and lean over the edge of the roof. Drop the barometer, timing its fall with a stopwatch. Then, using the formula $S = 1\backslash\ at^2$, calculate the height of the building.

At this point, I asked my colleague if he would give up. He conceded, and I gave the student almost full credit. I recalled the student had said he had other answers to the problem, so I asked him what they were.

"There are many ways to get the height of a building using a barometer," he said.

- "Take the barometer out on a sunny day. Measure the height of the barometer, the length of its shadow, and the length of the shadow of the building and, using proportions, calculate the height of the building.

- "Mark off the length of the barometer on the wall as you walk up the stairs. Then count the number of marks and multiply by the barometer's length.

- "Tie the barometer to the end of a string, swing it as a pendulum, and determine the value of g at the street level and at the top of the building, then calculate the difference between the two values of g.

"If you don't limit me to physics, there are many other answers, such as taking the barometer to the superintendent and offering to trade him the barometer in return for telling the height of the building."

I asked the student if he really didn't know the answer to the problem. He admitted he did but was fed up with instructors trying to teach him how to think instead of showing him the structure of the subject matter, and he regarded the exam mostly as a sham.

* * *

There are several problems with explicit criteria (or performance standards or rubrics) determined in advance. One problem is that *attention is directed toward the criteria and away from the student's actual performance.* The issue is where to place primary focus:

- Should the student work be in the foreground and generalized concepts of quality in the background? or
- Should criteria or standards be uppermost in the minds of assessors and what the student has actually done considered only where it links to the criteria or standards?

Use of explicit criteria tends to prioritize the criteria at the expense of attention to the particular features of student work.

A related problem is that *rigid use of criteria in scoring reduces flexibility.* Prespecified criteria and standards do not connect well with student work that is unique or different from what was expected by those who formulated the criteria and standards. When the student's work must be judged according to the criteria and not on its own merits, when the criteria are not well related to what the student has done, the student is likely to be undercredited for his or her accomplishment. In measurement terms, the inference of student accomplishment based on the score for the student work will be invalid—too low.

A third problem is that *criteria imply that all students' performances should conform to the criteria.* But should they? What about students who are capable of doing more than the criteria require, and who might do less than their best by trying to conform to the criteria by which they will be assessed? Conformity to criteria extends beyond the assessment. Many teachers feel that, to be fair to students, they should share grading criteria in advance. When there are criteria by which student performances will be evaluated, writers in all three paradigms tend to agree that advance sharing of criteria with students seems only fair.[6] Teachers share with students not only their own criteria but also state standards and rubrics.[7] Sharing criteria with students tends to standardize student performances. A study in Illinois, for example, found that students learned to write to the state's rubric: that prespecified criteria and standards had the effect of standardizing students' writing.[8] Teaching to the rubric is a dismaying variation on the theme of teaching to the test. The negative consequences of standardization or convergence of student thinking and products, dampening of creativity and self-expression, have not been thoroughly considered.

A fourth problem is that *a requirement to use criteria instead of professional judgment implies that teachers (or other assessors) cannot make complex judgments of quality on their own.* This is tantamount to claiming that teachers are incapable of higher-order thinking, evaluation being the final stage of Bloom's taxonomy of educational objectives:[9]

1. Knowledge
2. Comprehension
3. Application
4. Analysis

5. Synthesis

6. Evaluation

Explicit criteria are certainly helpful as reminders to pay attention to some aspects that may be important to good performance. But they are unhelpful when they encourage such unintended negative outcomes as standardizing student thinking and deprofessionalizing teachers and when they distract from aspects of actual performance. The harm done by such distraction is apparent in this critique of Britain's new national assessment:

> What did not seem to be grasped by policymakers, either initially or even after implementation was well under way, were the problems inherent in any system seeking to base its procedures on a frame of reference constructed on explicit attainment criteria. The characteristic and familiar conventions of norm-referencing led to outcomes being summarized in the opaque but manageable shorthand of marks, grades, and percentages. . . . The information on attainment which would help the struggling pupil to progress (one reason a teacher might keep a record) is going to be different in its form and level of detail.[10]

Preordinate, Emergent, or Negotiated Scoring Criteria

Another way to categorize scoring criteria and standards is based on when and by whom criteria are developed:

- **Preordinate** scoring criteria are determined in advance of the assessment, perhaps in advance of the learning opportunity.

- **Emergent** scoring criteria are determined during learning or assessment in response to what comes to be seen as important through direct experience or evidence.

- **Negotiated** scoring criteria are jointly determined by students and teachers (or other assessors), allowing for consideration of what students think is important about their own work.

Preordinate Criteria

Preordinate criteria determined in advance, as noted, can limit the personalization of assessment, directing attention more toward criteria and less toward the features and qualities of students' actual work. Measurement errors occur when students who meet criteria and standards in superficial, lackluster performances get higher scores than students who do better substantive work but in a way the criteria failed to anticipate. For example, one Vermont student might write a dull portfolio paper exhibiting purpose, organization, details, voice/tone, and usage/mechanics/grammar, whereas another student might write a paper featuring a compelling theme or argument well expressed in vivid or metaphoric language but get a lower mark on Vermont's 4-point measurement scale (standards) because of punctuation errors. Because the criteria on the scoring rubric fail to direct attention to interest, persuasiveness, and figurative language, assessment could yield scores that actually misrepresent both of these students' performances.

Such measurement errors are occurring. In 1997, one state offered a direct writing assessment prompt on the subject of why people should conserve water. The benchmark for the highest score on this assessment (i.e., the example paper to help assessors recognize when to award the highest score) listed strategies for conserving water rather than reasons to do so. That is, the state's "best paper" was irrelevant to the assigned topic. But the benchmark paper did conform to the criteria listed on the scoring rubric, which essentially gave credit for writing the traditional five-paragraph theme.[11] The benchmark paper had an opening paragraph in which a point was stated and three points of support listed, a subsequent paragraph on each of the three supporting points, and a summary conclusion.[12] In determining the quality of work in that paper, the *content* was ignored; the *form* was what counted because that's what the criteria required. This serious mistake could lead to statewide scoring errors as the benchmark paper guides assessors in their evaluations of student work.

Emergent Criteria

Emergent criteria allow teachers to respond to changes in lesson plans along the way, to respond to actual learning more than to anticipated learning, and to respond to serendipitous opportunities or calamities that affect the content of lessons. Emergent criteria also allow teachers to take into account insights like these:

> I see that no one is doing as well as I thought on plural and possessive nouns. Perhaps I didn't teach that well.

> Lots of students learned about research methods as well as about the solar system, which I hadn't expected. They deserve credit for that.

> Kerry took this idea and went off in a completely different direction from the one I anticipated. She's developed some real, specialized expertise.

Criteria can be stated toward the end of the lesson, instead of in advance, so that assessment is related to the curriculum *as experienced* rather than the curriculum *as planned*. Criteria can be stated even later, during assessment, as unanticipated features of student work are noticed and thought to deserve credit.

Negotiated Criteria

Negotiated criteria allow students opportunity to indicate what is important to them, including things they've learned that their teachers might not realize. It also gives students opportunity to consider what is important about what they are learning, to develop personal standards of quality, and to take responsibility for their own educations.

For criteria to be truly negotiated, assessors must be willing to share authority with students. It is not only that students must have an opportunity to share their ideas, but assessors must really listen and work to incorporate student's ideas into the assessment. This requires special care with students who are not very assertive or not very articulate. Care must also be taken to avoid either a loss of rigor or students' unrealistically high expectations of themselves. Negotiating criteria requires thoughtfulness, sensitivity, and skill.

Content and Performance Standards

As noted, explicit criteria can be preordinate or emergent and can be developed by teachers or negotiated between teachers and students. These aspects tell how, when, and by whom criteria might be developed. But *what* might the criteria look like?

Some disentangling of terminology may be helpful. Earlier, a distinction was made between criteria and standards:

Criteria: Statements telling *what* the test-taker must do, which aspects of performance will be considered in scoring

Examples: (from Vermont writing portfolios) Purpose, organization, details, voice/tone, usage/mechanics/grammar

Standards: Statements or indicators of *how good* the performance should be, or indicators of different levels of quality of performance

Examples: (from Vermont writing portfolios) Criteria in evidence extensively, frequently, sometimes, rarely

In many discussions, the terms criteria and standards are used interchangeably. Three different types of standards have become important in educational discourse:

- **Content standards:** Statements of what should be taught and what students should learn[13]

- **Performance standards:** Concrete examples and explicit definitions of what students must know and do to demonstrate proficiency[14]

- **Delivery** or **equity** or **opportunity standards:** Criteria for assessing the adequacy of resources provided to students.[15]

Content standards tend to be more general and more idealized than performance standards, telling what we hope students will learn or articulating aims we hope teachers are striving toward in instruction. But there is confusion in the use of these terms. Frequently, personnel working with large-scale assessment programs describe these programs as having content standards but, on inspection, the standards sometimes describe very specific performances and the levels by which they will be judged. That is, the so-called content standards are actually performance standards.[16]

Sometimes standards and rubrics (or scoring criteria) are confused. Scoring criteria, often presented as rubrics, are more specific statements that may operationalize performance standards. The Vermont writing portfolio Analytic Assessment Guide was an example of a rubric (see Table 4.3). Other state writing rubrics show the influence of the Vermont rubric on other programs.

Benchmark is another term used in different ways, creating confusion. Some state assessment programs use the term benchmark to refer to performance levels, rendering the term synonymous to performance standards. Other programs use the term to refer to **exemplars,** which some others refer to as **range-finding papers.** An example of the latter can be found in Vermont, where assessors were provided a benchmark paper corresponding to each cell in the Analytic Assessment Guide. Vermont's fourth-grade benchmarks for the criterion *purpose* at the standards (performance levels) *extensively* and *rarely* are given in the following paragraphs.

Grade 4 Benchmark for Criterion *"Purpose" and Standard "Extensively"*

> Being a parent is not a piece of cake! Kids can be so bad! They act up all the time and they talk back! They say no and they don't even obey. Parents can't go to the parties anymore because they have to stay home with their kids. Keeping track of your kids takes more time away from a parents plans. Parents have to earn more money. Parents have to buy clothes, diapers, food, toys, shoes, blankets, and more and more stuff. They even have to do all kinds of chores because they have to clean up all the babies messes. You have to remember it is not a piece of cake being a parent!!

Grade 4 Benchmark for Criterion *"Purpose" and Standard "Rarely"*

> WHEN MY DAD WENT TO THE HOSTAPIL
> The date was Dec. 8, 1990 I HATED!! Michelyne, Dannielle, and I stayed at the Camp's house over night. It was O.K. Michelyne cooked dinner (don't tell this but it was gross!!) other wise it was good!! On the other hand dad was on his way to the hostapil , it took 2 hours to get there.

> Source: Vermont Department of Education (1991)

Understanding these terms is important because much of the grand conversation about assessment and educational reform focuses on standards. "High standards for all" has become a common watchword and national standards a prominent focus. The National Education Goals Panel (NEGP) was established by Congress to set educational standards and to develop a system of national assessments. The National Assessment Governing Board (NAGB), which steers the National Assessment of Educational Progress (NAEP), was recently suggested as the overseer of a national test now described as voluntary[17] but unlikely to be so in practice.[18] Professional organizations have developed standards in content areas, the first of these being the National Council of Teachers of Mathematics.[19]

State-mandated performance testing programs are increasingly standards based. Some states have set standards as the first step in developing their performance assessment systems, with the assessments intended to measure performance related to the standards. Some states had implemented performance assessments before the standards movement; most of these have developed or are developing standards and checking the alignment of their assessments to their new standards.[20]

There has been little critical consideration as to whether we *should* have standards-based assessment, whether we *should* expect all kids to learn the same things to a particular level of proficiency.[21] Great confidence has been expressed in the notion of high standards for all, with too little concern that students with inferior educational opportunities might be punished twice—once by poor schooling and a second time by exams that yield scores that foreclose on students' educational and life opportunities.[22]

Analytic or Holistic Scoring

Scoring is also distinguished by whether it is analytic or holistic. In **analytic** scoring, different features or parts of a performance are evaluated separately. Judgments of the quality of the parts are synthesized or aggregated—often added or averaged—to obtain a score or grade. In **holistic** scoring, the quality of the performance as a whole is emphasized rather than of assessment of its parts. Of course, some aspects of the performance may be especially praised or noted as needing improvement, but the focus is on the quality of the performance overall with attention to the contributions to the whole made by different aspects. The underlying assumption is that the whole is greater than (or, at least, different from) the sum of its parts.

In analytic assessment, the criteria that form the basis for judging the quality of a student's work may or may not be prespecified. However, scoring is much more likely to be analytic rather than holistic when criteria are prespecified, each criterion directing attention to a specific aspect of the work. For example, even if a teacher in Vermont were asked to score a portfolio entry holistically rather than analytically using the state's criteria, the criteria would inevitably direct her attention to purpose, organization, details, voice/tone, and usage/mechanics/grammar. Her overall score would reflect a synthesis judgment as to how well the student performed on the five criteria more than a holistic assessment of overall quality, which might reflect criteria other than those prespecified by the state.

Rather than criteria that break student work down to components, holistic assessment may be guided by questions such as the following:

What achievement has the student demonstrated in this work? What is the level of accomplishment? What contributes to (and what undermines) the quality?

These are general questions requiring attention to both the overall quality of the work and to specific contributory aspects. The assessor details the aspects of interest—whether positive or negative, present or absent—based on what the student has actually done, rather than on some prior expectation which may or may not fit with the student's performance.

Ipsative Assessment

As defined earlier, ipsative assessment involves judging a student's performance on the basis of his or her relative strengths and weaknesses, skills and knowledge, progress over time, opportunity to learn, interests, goals, academic and personal background, and any other known factors that may affect performance.[23] Ipsative assessment does not focus on whether a student has learned a given curriculum, and it does not facilitate comparisons among students as much as it generates a fuller understanding of each student and an appreciation of his or her unique accomplishments. In contrast to other assessment strategies, ipsative assessment is more personalized:

Assessment Paradigm	Assessment Strategy
Personalized paradigm	*Ipsative assessment:* (not standardized, not normative) "How well does this student understand science?"
Contextual paradigm	*Curriculum-based assessment:* (might or might not be criterion referenced, standards based, standardized, normative) "How well did this student learn science in class?"
Psychometric paradigm	*Standardized assessment:* (typically normative, might or might not also be criterion referenced, standards based) "How well does this student's science achievement compare with that of other students at the same grade level?"

Assessment Focus and Purpose

The three approaches feature different foci useful for different purposes. The psychometric paradigm aims for test-based comparisons of student performances; the contextual paradigm offers curriculum-based tests to determine what students have learned from the educational opportunity their teachers have provided; the personalized paradigm foregrounds the student, backgrounds the curriculum, and eschews interstudent comparison. It is a question of where to direct the spotlight.

Ipsative assessment targets individuals and their achievement more than comparing students' performances, as norm-referenced assessments do, or determining what students have learned from the curricular opportunities presented to them, as curriculum-based assessments do. Curriculum-based assessment may note what the student failed to learn of the curriculum presented. Standardized assessment will focus on the student's rank within a group of test-takers more than on what the student knows and can do.

- Standardized assessment asks the question, "Which child knows more?"

- Curriculum-based assessment asks the question, "What did this child learn in class?"

- Ipsative assessment asks the question, "What does this child know?"

In ipsative assessment, the focus is on the student, with strong reference to the domain of interest. There may be some reference to the curriculum, but ipsative assessment works on the possibility that the student may know more about the domain than was offered in the classroom—in which case a curriculum-based assessment will undercredit, underrepresent, and underestimate what the student knows, whereas a personalized or ipsative assessment may detect this additional achievement. In ipsative assessment, there is little or no reference to other students, so little opportunity to compare. The difference in focus among these assessment strategies is illustrated in Figures 4.1 and 4.2.

Effects of Explicit, Predetermined, Specific Performance Criteria

Personalized assessment assumes that different students might not only perform differently but also might demonstrate entirely different skills and knowledge in unique ways. Preset criteria and highly specific criteria usually lack the flexibility needed to credit a wide range of student performances. Without flexibility, students who perform in unique ways are typically penalized for failing to meet the usual expectations—even in

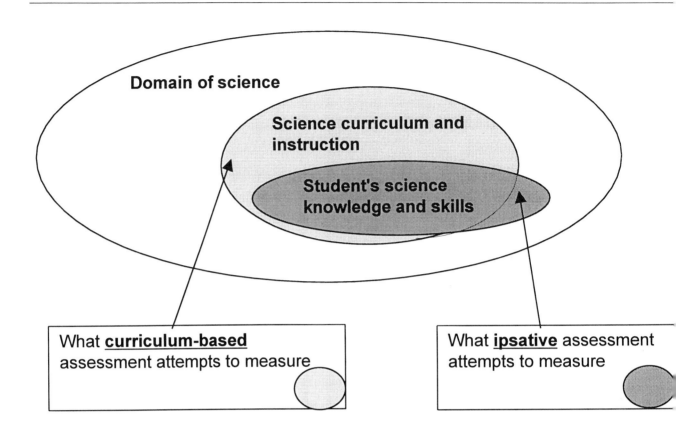

Figure 4.1. Difference in Focus Between Ipsative and Curriculum-Based Assessment

cases where close examination might reveal they actually exceeded the expectations.

The following is an example of *a very specific performance criterion* from a state performance assessment:

> Student correctly makes two graphs displaying the information given in the question.[24]

A criterion such as this requires a student to take a specific approach in demonstrating knowledge and skills. It denies the student an opportunity to decide how to demonstrate achievement. What if a student was very knowledgeable about the topic of the question but not about graphing? What if a student had a better way to show his or her knowledge than by using a graph? What if a student's knowledge on the topic in question was more complex that two graphs could reveal? Requiring a particular type of performance can lead to assessment that underestimates a student's actual level of knowledge and skills, yielding a score too low to support a valid inference of the student's actual achievement.

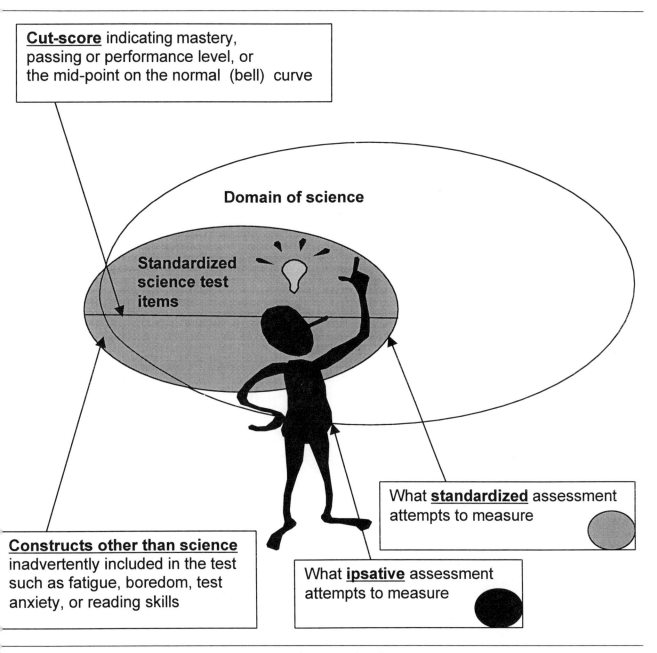

Cut-score indicating mastery, passing or performance level, or the mid-point on the normal (bell) curve

Domain of science

Standardized science test items

Constructs other than science inadvertently included in the test such as fatigue, boredom, test anxiety, or reading skills

What **standardized** assessment attempts to measure

What **ipsative** assessment attempts to measure

Figure 4.2. Difference in Focus Between Ipsative and Standardized Assessment

General criteria that are broad enough for use with a variety of evidence of achievement are more useful for ipsative assessments to which students might respond in different ways. For example, the following is *a general performance criterion* from another state performance assessment:

Responses demonstrate a sustained sequence of events with a logical progression of ideas.[25]

To meet this criterion, students might do any of a number of things: construct a timeline, write a narrative describing the influence of one event on another, draw a cartoon, prepare an outline or a flowchart, or dramatize the events. There is flexibility for tailoring the assessment to many types of performance that may seem useful to the student or to the assessors.

Not at all an indication of diminished rigor in the assessment, this less specific criterion requires more effort by both the student and the assessors. Some difficult but interesting questions are likely to surface:

What do I know about this subject?

Do I know enough? What else should I learn? Am I ready to be assessed?

How can I demonstrate to assessors what I know and can do?

The student must think about what he or she knows, what type of performance might best demonstrate that, whether more information should be gathered or reviewed or learned. Note the opportunity for self-assessment, self-initiated learning, and development of responsibility and personal standards. Note that such personalization promotes interest and motivation and that it connects learning and assessing by making assessment educative. All this with no loss of rigor—this assessment requires more thinking and effort because the student must detect and define the parameters of the problem, must devise a plan of attack, and must evaluate what constitutes completion and success. More specificity or predefinition of a problem or of criteria for a solution means these critical cognitive processes are completed by others before the student encounters the problem, making the student's task both easier and less engaging.

Not only must students engage in more complex thinking when presented with ill-defined problems,[26] but assessors also are called to a more rigorous effort. Assessors must be flexible enough to respond to whatever performance the student devises, prepared to judge whether and how well the performance provides evidence of learning, and ready to search for meaning in the performance and for appropriate inferences based on the evidence. Together, student and assessors may negotiate the type of performance expected, or the assessors may permit the student to decide.

If individualized standards are to be used to judge the quality of the student's performance, rather than general standards for every performance, questions will also arise as to which standards or how high the standards should be set for a particular student:

What would be a reasonable expectation of quality of performance?

How can I, as a student, be sure my performance is high quality?

How can I, as an assessor, be sure I recognize high quality in different types of performances?

Individualized standards might be formal statements—written expectations for the student, perhaps negotiated with the student. Or individualized standards might be intuitive and unstated in any formal way, based on experience of the student's capability and circumstances and on the difficulty and importance of the task undertaken.

We cannot measure everything a student has learned. No score or percentile or grade or narrative can capture and represent all that a child knows and can do. No standard—general, task specific, individualized, implicit, or explicit—prevents measurement error. Assessors may attend to some learning more than others, underemphasize salient conditions, fail to recognize or prioritize or legitimize some accomplishments or circumstances. Assessment is a matter of inference, of judgments based on evidence. Good educational measurement requires strong evidence, preferably evidence gathered by different means over a period of time: multi-method assessment. The better the evidence, the more probable an assessor will make accurate or valid inferences of a student's achievement.

Promoting Deep Understanding and Valid Inferences of Student Achievement

Questions such as those listed above reach into the heart of assessment. They press for deep understanding of students' knowledge and abilities, for valid inferences of their achievement. They press for more than good measurement—they also help students become more self-aware, better able to recognize their own progress, better able to identify gaps in their education. They encourage students to take responsibility for their education, motivate them to learn what they themselves see they don't yet know, and stimulate them to set personal standards of quality. They help assessors do more than merely assign a score. Ipsative assessment keeps open the thinking and the conversation about what a student has achieved, not foreclosing on deep understanding by assigning a final score or grade before thinking and focused discussion.

But what if assessors disagree? In normative assessment, **reliability**—consistency of a student's scores on equivalent measures or from different scorers—is crucial because comparisons are problematic if scores fluctuate from day to day, test to (equivalent) test, or scorer to scorer. So consensus is needed about assessment criteria and standards, and training of assessors is needed to apply these criteria and standards as uniformly as possible. (Other reasons why reliability is important will be examined in a later section on validity and reliability.)

In ipsative assessment, personalized and contextualized understanding of the student is crucial. These assessments are not destabilized when scorers disagree. Rather, disagreements about quality of performance are likely to be productive for discussion and, consequently, greater understanding. Differences in assessors' criteria and standards, made apparent to students in feedback, are likely to assist students in developing their own performance standards for self-assessment. Differences in assessment criteria and standards are more authentic than consensus, more reflective of a pluralistic society and its often conflicting demands. In ipsative assessment, commentary and even argument are important, whereas scores and the reliability of scores are sometimes—not always—unnecessary.[27]

As will be discussed more fully later, agreement among assessors is needed so there can be confidence in assessments, especially if assessment results are to be used in high-stakes decision making, such as whether a student will be permitted to graduate from high school. But the need for confidence in scores should be balanced against the need for strong understanding of student achievement—valid inferences of achievement. The relationship between validity and reliability is more complex and more conflicted than has often been recognized.

Practical implications of the contrast between normative and ipsative assessment strategies are immense. For example, *normatively assessed portfolios* would likely involve

- Specification of portfolio entries and, perhaps, of organization and formatting
- Grades for portfolios and/or portfolio entries
- Rubrics stating criteria and standards for grades

By contrast, *ipsatively assessed portfolios* would likely involve

- Student-selected and/or teacher-student negotiated selection of portfolio entries; entries submitted by parents or other faculty and staff might also be included
- Narrative evaluations, commentaries, or reflections about portfolio entries by the student (self-assessment), teacher, and possibly, peers, parents, and other faculty and staff—or the portfolio itself rather than evaluative comments or grades—might serve as evidence of the student's level of achievement
- Personalized criteria and standards, perhaps unstated, devised to reflect the student's interests, abilities, opportunities, and goals

Scorers

Authentic and performance assessment offer special benefits, and they take time. The benefits often increase and the time becomes more manageable when the authority for assessing is shared. The most important bene-

ficiaries of sharing assessment responsibilities are students, but others
who may be asked to judge the quality of student achievement include

> other teachers,
>
> other school staff persons,
>
> administrators,
>
> other students in the same classroom or other classrooms,
>
> the student's parents,
>
> other parents,
>
> members of the community, and
>
> members of the school board or other governing bodies.

Students may work individually to assess their own performance (self-
evaluation) or that of their classmates (peer assessment). Or they may work
in teams to assess some of the work they and their classmates are expected
to produce. Student assessment teams may work with the teacher to devise criteria or, once they have gained experience, may be asked to draft
criteria for teacher review or for immediate use. Sharing of assessment authority has highly beneficial effects, including the following.

- Students behave and come to perceive themselves as professionals
  (or professional-like), thinking about what counts as quality and
  developing personal standards of quality. Students develop adult-
  like and professional-like skills and dispositions.
- As students develop their own standards of quality, their own work
  typically improves, sometimes dramatically.
- Students develop a capacity and comfort level in articulating their
  work to others. (Consider how helpful this can be for college and
  job applications.)
- Students invest in and take responsibility for their own learning.
- Students get ideas by looking at the work of their peers, increasing
  their range of endeavor, their motivation, and their respect for each
  other.
- Students experience teamwork and the value of feedback from critical friends—collegiality.
- Students develop competence at assessment.
- Teachers are relieved of some time-consuming obligations of using
  authentic assessment.

Sharing authority for assessment often raises some questions teachers
and others would do well to consider in advance, such as

Whose criteria and standards should be used?

Should all students be expected to meet identical criteria and standards, although their interests, goals, and opportunities are different?

How well do assessors need to know students to be able to judge their performance?

What if assessors disagree? Should consensus be forced? Or could we honor differences of opinion, different standards?

Different aspects of the assessment process can be assigned to different persons, as Table 4.6 suggests.

Whether, when, how, and with whom to share assessment authority are considerations for flexible, adaptive practice rather than questions with uniform answers. In this regard, as with assessment generally, best practice appears to be a commitment to thoughtful struggle rather than attainment of perfection.

Self-Assessment

In the psychometric assessment paradigm, the pivotal task of scoring is reserved to machines or to trained scorers, usually persons who know nothing of the students whose work they evaluate. Distance from learners coupled with assessment's strong influence on learning contexts: This combination has sometimes been described as education (or educational reform) by remote control. In the contextual assessment paradigm, responsibility for scoring falls to teachers, a proximal relocation which capitalizes on local knowing-in-action[28] and familiarity with students. In the personalized assessment paradigm, the drive to the heart of the matter reaches its ultimate destination by actualizing the understanding that the most important assessment that can occur is self-assessment.

We lament student apathy, lack of personal investment in education, willingness to cheat—without acknowledging our complicity in depriving students of opportunities to exercise judgment and choice. We deny them responsibility, then reproach them when they seem irresponsible. This situation may be redressed by curbing our proclivities for control and authority and offering guidance and insight instead. Sharing authority, letting students be players rather than objects or outcomes, continues a move in the right direction, away from students as passive receivers of knowledge to active learners. Not only cognitive, the move toward personalization is also political—students seen not only as framers of understanding but also as makers of educational decisions and judgments.

Students who have been granted real voice in curriculum and assessment processes tend to respond with intelligence, responsibility, and determination, as the examples in Part 2 showcase. This is true not only of

TABLE 4.6 Sharing Assessment Authority With Students: A Planning Instrument

Who Will?	Set Criteria and Standards	Award Grade	Offer Commentary or Feedback
Teacher			
Student			
Student pairs or groups			
Student teams			
Other			

"most likely to succeed" candidates but also for students who have experienced failure, even given up. We have been too willing to use assessment to tell students what they don't know, that they're not as accomplished as their peers, that they don't deserve the opportunities provided by this program or that school. By making them integral, central to assessment, we can not only honor their opinions, their achievements, and their aspirations but also cultivate identification and effort toward their goals and metacognitive monitoring and self-evaluation of progress. For too many students, education has been a tragedy, and testing is part of the reason why. But the opportunity exists for assessment to turn educational victims into the stars of their own scripts.

Formal self-assessment is uncommon in education. Students need opportunities to develop skills and to realize that their judgments really matter, that self-assessment is not pro forma, that their opinions will not be praised and then excluded from important decisions. They also need help in engaging in the intellectual effort to assess achievement, not merely to describe effort or feelings. Teachers need opportunities, too, to learn from experience how to make thoughtful decisions as to when and how to incorporate student judgment into assessment (see Figure 4.3).

1. Young children or nonwriters can be asked to describe orally or to represent pictorially their judgments of the quality of their work. For example:

> Draw the rest of the face so that it shows how you feel about your work.

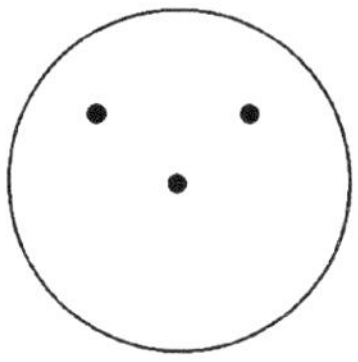

2. Students new to self-evaluation may feel hesitant. Asking them to do just a little initially, then gradually become accustomed to self-assessment may help. Using small forms or bits of paper—stick-on notes or file cards, for instance—may lower early feelings of intimidation with the task. Students could later be asked to review their brief early words and to replace them or add to them later with a fuller evaluation or a description of progress since then. A related option: Peers could be encouraged to offer one-word descriptions or evaluations, which could help to stimulate self-evaluation writing.

> Write one word (or an adjective or phrase) to describe your level of satisfaction with your work.

3. Sentence completion forms can stimulate and focus thinking on achievement by offering stems such as

> • In this work, I hoped to _____
>
> • What I feel I actually accomplished is _____
>
> • I am satisfied with this aspect: _____
>
> • I was able to do more than I thought I could with this aspect:
>
> _____
>
> • I think I still need to work on _____
>
> • What I learned as a result of this work is _____
>
> • Next (or next time), I am planning to _____
>
> • I would give this a grade of _____ because _____
>
> _____

Figure 4.3. Self-Assessment Ideas

4. Self-assessment ideas that are interesting or motivating in themselves may be used to get started or with discouraged learners. For example:

Choose a song title (or movie title, book title, postage stamp, cartoon character) to express your thoughts about your work.

- *'S Wonderful*
- *I Can't Get No Satisfaction*
- *I Get By With a Little Help From My Friends*
- Other:

Tell why you chose that title.

---

5. Teachers may ask students to evaluate their work on particular aspects or criteria. Or teacher and students together can identify criteria of interest for both to consider in assessing. Or students can be asked to identify criteria of individual interest and relevance. Or students may be asked to self-assess without reference to prespecified criteria, but rather to explain or justify their judgments. Criteria might include something like the following:

Understanding of the three branches of government

Understanding of the legislative process (how a bill becomes law)

Understanding of judicial process

Understanding of executive obligations and limitations

Familiarity with the officials who represent my community

Familiarity with my rights and how to exercise them

Familiarity with current events nationally

Familiarity with current events locally

Theme of story (Interesting? Well-developed?)

Characters (Believable? Multidimensional?)

Plot (Coherent? Far-fetched? Good vehicle for theme and characters?)

Beginning (Attention getting? Sets the stage for the rest?)

Ending (Meaningful? Abrupt? Realistic?)

Language and style (Clear? Vivid? Memorable? Fluent?)

Other

Figure 4.3. Continued

Summary of Scoring Choices

One way to summarize the ideas about scoring presented here and the relationships among these ideas is by noticing how scoring systems differ in the degree to which assessors' judgments will be criterial or case-by-case.

Criteria can be preordinate or emergent or negotiated. Criteria might be implicit but, for formal assessment, are usually explicit. Criterial judgments can be based on normative standards (relative to other students' performances) or on content standards or on both. Content standards tell what a student should know; performance standards tell what and how well a student must do in demonstrating what he or she knows. Some standards feature grades or numerical or scalar scores, some standards have descriptive anchors, and some have both. In an analytic evaluation, aspects of a performance are taken separately, then combined for a final score or judgment.

By contrast, **case-by-case** judgments are tailored to individual performances; thus, they are more likely to be personalized, ipsative decisions. Case-by-case judgments might be based on explicit or implicit criteria, but these judgments are very likely to emerge from student performance (emergent criteria) rather than from predetermined standards (preordinate criteria). Case-by-case judgments are more likely than criterial judgments to be holistic assessments of the quality of the performance as a whole, rather than analytic assessments of how well aspects of a performance satisfy criteria and how these subassessments aggregate into a final score.

Another way to summarize the information presented here is as a series of decisions, which may be helpful for readers who are planning to develop performance assessment systems. Decision points:

- Whether to assess

- What type of items or formats to use

- If achievement is to be assessed, which theoretical approach to take (or, stated another way, whether to standardize assessments across curricula, to link assessments to a particular curriculum, or to individualize assessments)

- Whether to determine quality of performance based on comparison to other test-takers, comparison to standards or criteria, or without comparison

- If quality of performance is to be based on standards or criteria, whether to state criteria and/or standards formally (explicit) or not (implicit)

- If assessment is to be based on explicit criteria, *how early* in the process to state the criteria and/or standards or to develop a rubric

- If assessment is to be based on standards, *how specifically* stated the standards for judging performance will be

- If assessment is to be based on criteria and/or standards, *who* will determine the criteria and/or standards

Sequencing of decisions might involve an order similar to that found in Figure 4.4.

Recognition of the many options available and decisions to be made in developing an assessment system can help clarify assessment purposes and can better connect assessment to education. Informed and thoughtful decision making can avoid some of the conflicts embedded in some current assessment systems.

Conflicts in Assessment Systems

When strategies and paradigms are mismatched, avoidable conflicts and limitations bedevil assessment systems. When practical decisions are made without recognizing the underlying theory, mismatches like the following can and do happen.

- Writing portfolios intended to encourage and to assess student self-expression are standardized by use of a rubric. As students become familiar with the assessment system, they increasingly incorporate the rubric's criteria in their writing. As a result, student writings start to look similar (standardized), unintentionally thwarting a basic purpose of writing, self-expression.

Misconceptions are unintentionally encouraged. As students formulate their notions about what writing is and what constitutes quality in writing, they are influenced by the narrowness of the implied definition of good writing to be found in the rubric.

Validity is unintentionally compromised. Those students who demonstrate creative self-expression rather than writing to the rubric are penalized. Even when they do high-quality work, if their work exhibits a different kind of quality than that anticipated by the rubric, they receive low scores. Meantime, students who minimally meet the rubric's requirements with dull papers are rewarded with undeserved high scores.[29]

- Projects are assigned in which students undertake authentic inquiry,[30] which results in personalized knowledge and understandings. But assessment of the projects involves comparison to a standard, the same standard for all. This facilitates comparison to other students' performances, but the uniqueness of the projects suggests the need for differentiated assessment standards and obstructs comparison among students. Differentiated assessment standards would also allow assessors to take

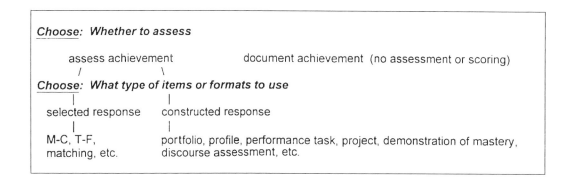

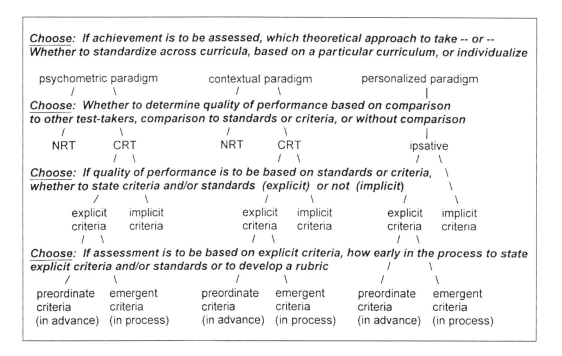

Choose: If assessment is to be based on standards, whether standards will tell how well
the test-taker must perform, what the test-taker must know, or what the test-taker will be
provided before testing -- or -- How specifically stated will the standards for judging
performance be

performance standards   content standards   delivery standards
(how well the test-taker   (what the test-taker   (what the test-taker is
must perform, e.g., rubrics)   must know)   provided beforehand)

Choose: If assessment is to be based on criteria and/or standards, who will determine the
criteria and/or standards

teachers (and/or other assessors)   assessors and students together

Figure 4.4. Summary of Scoring Choices
NOTE: NRT = norm-referenced test; CRT = criterion-referenced test.

into account the fact that students encountered different working circumstances or different availability and quality of resources.

- Performance tasks are administered to students in which they construct individual responses. Each student response is scored by two trained raters. To achieve an acceptable level of agreement among assessors (interrater reliability), the raters are trained to look for certain aspects (criteria) and to judge according to predetermined standards. If two raters disagree about the score for a student response, an arbiter decides the score. In trying to ensure agreement, raters and arbiters make some joint decisions about what will distinguish between different performance levels (performance standards). Sometimes, these distinctions bear little relation to the quality of a student's performance; whether the answer includes a particular word (used correctly or not) may decide whether a student's response is considered satisfactory.[31]

These and other kinds of mismatches suggest that the coherence of a performance assessment system requires a good fit between theory, strategy, and technique. New assessment techniques become distorted when forced into an old, often fundamentally hostile assessment paradigm.

Moreover, new assessment techniques are expansionist, whereas large-scale assessments typically employ reductionist strategies. That is, techniques like portfolios *expand* the database of student performance by collecting many samples of a student's work, much evidence of his or her achievement. This stands in contrast to standardized, norm-referenced, multiple-choice achievement testing where indications of achievement are *reduced* to a score. Individualized performances, constructed-response items, and assessments that elicit elaborate demonstrations of achievement fit better with assessment strategies that respond to these performances with complex, elaborated, individualized feedback rather than cut-scores or placement decisions.

Studies of both small- and large-scale performance assessments[32] suggest that some important benefits of new assessment techniques are undermined by expanded scale and by traditional paradigmatic assumptions.[33] The unhappy perspective gained:

1. Regardless of technique or item type, large-scale assessments are more likely to follow the psychometric paradigm because a larger number of test-takers presses for systematization and standardization.

2. Regardless of test format—multiple-choice items or performance tasks or portfolios—systematization and standardization obstruct curriculum sensitivity and student sensitivity in assessment. Standardizing alternative assessment techniques produces paradigmatic conflict. This limits the capacity of new assessment

techniques to render complete and sensitive portrayals of student achievement and to inform curriculum planners.

The effects of paradigmatic conflict wound students, teachers, and schools in the high-stakes tactics increasingly deployed in state-level performance assessment systems.[34]

There are several potential skirmish points for paradigmatic conflict:

Conflict Between Assessment Paradigm and Curriculum

Example: In Chicago, four schools in the Lake View Education and Arts Partnership (LEAP), described in Part 2, have worked since 1993 to develop instructional units taught by teacher-artist teams integrating academics and fine arts. These units involve complex thinking and demonstrations of achievement, development of cross-curricular knowledge, and team-developed curriculum-based assessments. LEAP has been recognized for its accomplishment by Harvard's Arts Survive as one of eight "promising" arts education programs in the country.

But one LEAP school has remained on Chicago's infamous "watch list" because student scores have not been high enough on the state-mandated test (Illinois Goals Assessment Program, IGAP) and the city-mandated test (Iowa Test of Basic Skills, ITBS). The inference manifested in the recognition from Harvard is of exceptionally fine teaching and learning. The inference manifested in the watch list is of inadequate teaching and learning. LEAP schools are under heavy pressure to teach to the tests, which are grounded in a behaviorist assessment paradigm in conflict with LEAP's constructivist curriculum. The tests assess performance on isolated facts; LEAP's integrated curriculum lessons favor personally integrated knowledge and complex understandings.

Conflict Between Assessment Paradigm and Pedagogy

Example: Emily Dickinson Elementary School in Redmond, Washington, also noted in Part 2, underwent thorough educational reform planned and implemented by a dedicated faculty and staff. After becoming perhaps the most inclusive school in the state and adopting multiage classrooms and developmentally appropriate, inquiry-based, and cooperative learning, the school sought an assessment method harmonious with the student-initiated and collaborative pedagogical techniques favored by the faculty. Realizing that standardized multiple-choice tests were unlikely to reflect the student motivation and learning for which the school had been recognized and admired, personnel began work in 1992 to develop an alternative system of assessment and accountability. This effort was supported by the Lake Washington School District.

Conflict Between Assessment Paradigm and Assessment Techniques

Example: In 1991-1992, after a year of pilot testing, Vermont promoted the first statewide adoption of portfolios in the country. Portfolios as a technique offer outstanding opportunity for ipsative assessment and self-awareness. But Vermont's portfolios were highly standardized, with the state determining the type and number of portfolio entries, the criteria by which they were judged, and the performance standards that indicated quality of performance. The portfolio system's constraints allowed little opportunity to document a student's progress over time, relative strengths and weaknesses, academic opportunity or background, interests or goals. An ipsative technique with great promise for personalization had been limited by its embedding in a standardized system operating largely within the psychometric paradigm. This new-wine-in-old-skins type of conflict is typical of state-mandated performance assessment systems.[35]

Conflict Between Assessment Paradigm and Scale

Not only in state performance assessment systems does scale overwhelm personalized or curriculum-based assessment possibilities. School size makes a difference. Example: Demonstrations of mastery were found to be highly personalized, rigorous, and meaningful at little Walden III High School in Racine, Wisconsin[36] but impersonal, superficial, and even pointless at much larger Eastern High School in Louisville, Kentucky.[37]

At Walden, each senior was required to demonstrate knowledge and skills in 16 subjects over the course of a semester to a team of assessors that convened and reconvened solely for the purpose of evaluating that one student's readiness for life after high school. The assessors developed deep understanding of the student's competence. At Eastern, each senior was required to make one brief presentation to the student body assembled in the auditorium at the end of the year. That this was a pro forma exercise was suggested by a teacher's recollection that one senior had elected to demonstrate how to make a peanut butter and jelly sandwich.

Conflict Between Assessment Purposes

Example: Washington's 1992 Senate Substitute Bill 5953 established four purposes for the state's new assessment system (not yet implemented), which was required by law to include performance assessments. Two of these purposes, which are common to many large-scale assessment systems, are mutually obstructive. The assessment system was to produce and report (1) individual results indicating the achievement of each student, and (2) aggregated results indicating the quality of educational programs.

Aggravated by public reporting, which humiliates low-scoring schools, and by making school funding partially contingent on aggregated scores, assessment systems like this are vulnerable to the same "score pollution"[38] that compromises the validity of inferences based on standardized multiple-choice tests. Where schools are funded and teachers and administrators judged on the basis of individual scores, the same personnel who make local test administration decisions are under pressure to produce acceptable scores. When school personnel are pressed hard enough by high stakes they consider unfair or injurious to their students and their professional status, they tend to succumb to the pressure to what has regularly been called, in blame-the-victims style, "cheating."

Both the conflictedness of purpose and the pressure-cooker environment could be avoided by (1) using for purposes of educational program evaluation and accountability **matrix-sampled assessment** in which no student takes the full test or receives an individual score, in which student scores cannot be aggregated at the school or district level, but in which longitudinal and regional trends can be revealed; and (2) reserving **full census assessment** for reporting individual achievement, refusing to aggregate individual scores, thereby foiling the otherwise inevitable attempts to judge program performance on the basis of aggregated individual performance, an invalid use of individual scores against which the measurement community has repeatedly warned.[39]

Conflict Between Educational Goals and Assessment Policy

Example: The Waco Independent School District's publicized formal goals are as follows:

All students in all student groups will pass [the Texas Assessment of Academic Skills] at 90% in reading, writing, and mathematics.

All students and each student group will have 99% stay in school.

Student attendance rate for Grades K-12 will be at 97%.

Waco students will demonstrate an exemplary academic performance in comparison to state, national, and international standards.[40]

The history of large-scale testing in the United States for the past 30 years has repeatedly shown that setting a high cut-score or performance level, such as Waco's 90% requirement,[41] leads to increased dropouts. Can students in Waco, 76% of whom belong to minority groups[42] and nearly 80% of whom qualify for free- or reduced-price lunch,[43] buck that trend? Texas has posted gains in test scores and reduced dropouts—results that some have called impressive,[44] but others have attributed the gains to subversion of the curriculum[45] and such pressures as faculty dismissal, financial reward for high scores, and denial of high school diplomas. Even proponents have called these inducements "a sledgehammer."[46]

* * *

Where the fit is poor between assessment purposes and paradigms, or between purposes or paradigms and techniques, conflict is embedded in the system. Caught in these unintended conflicts or overwhelmed by scale, the benefits of new assessment techniques are cut short. Ipsative assessment is frequently jeopardized by scale, by the thinking and habits of an old paradigm, by cross-purposes. The student as an individual can be nearly as lost to view as in standardized, multiple-choice, norm-referenced testing. The problem of fitting together assessment purposes and paradigms and techniques is essentially an issue of focus. Should we focus on the test—try to find out where students rank related to group performance on the test construct or content? Should we focus on the curriculum—try to find out how well students have learned what was taught? Should we focus on the student—try to find out what he or she knows and can do?

Validity and Reliability

Inevitably, a discussion of assessment centers on the psychometric principles of validity and reliability, especially validity. Although other factors such as equity and feasibility are important, the quality of an assessment of achievement rests on its ability to support valid inferences of a test-taker's achievement.

Recognizing the problems engendered by paradigmatic conflict embedded in new assessment systems, some advocates of alternative assessment have suggested that the basic measurement principles of validity and reliability are either inappropriate or in need of adaptation. I agree with those who hold that validity and reliability are just as important for new as for traditional approaches to assessment.

I will argue that validity *improves* in rigorous and coherent personalized assessment systems, that the inferences of a student's achievement are enhanced by focus on the student's individual achievement rather than on rankings or a test or even on the curriculum, and that we are bound to understand an individual's achievement better if we focus on individual achievement.[47]

Validity

The basic idea of validity is expressed in the question, "On the basis of the student's performance on this assessment, can I infer what he or she knows about the subject tested?" Two similar, current technical definitions of validity:

> Validity is an overall evaluation of the degree to which evidence and theory support the interpretations of test scores entailed by specific uses of tests. As such, validity is the most important consideration in test development and evaluation. The process of validation involves accumulating evidence to provide a sound scientific basis for the proposed score interpretations. It is the interpretations of test scores required by specific uses that are evaluated, not the test itself. Thus, when test scores are used or interpreted in more than one way, each intended interpretation must be evaluated.[48]

> Validity is an integrated evaluative judgment of the degree to which empirical evidence and theoretical rationales support the *adequacy* and *appropriateness* of *inferences* and *actions* based on test scores or other modes of assessment.... [V]alidity is an inductive summary of both the existing evidence for and the potential consequences of score interpretation and use. Hence, what is to be validated is not the test or observation device as such but the inferences derived from test scores of other indicators—inferences about score meaning or interpretation and about the implications for action that the interpretation entails.[49]

An example of *validity:* Pat, a good student who has made As in science every term for eight years and who won last year's science fair, earns a high score on a science assessment. From this score, knowing nothing else about Pat and concentrating solely on the score, we might correctly infer that Pat has an excellent grasp of science. An example of **in***validity:* A world-renowned scientist earns a low score on the same test, which is given in English, a language the scientist does not speak. From this score, knowing nothing else about the scientist and concentrating solely on the score, we might incorrectly infer that the scientist's knowledge of science is poor.

Notice that it is neither the test nor the scores that are valid or invalid, but the **inferences** based on the scores that are more or less valid. Notice also that validity is not dichotomous, that inferences are not simply valid or invalid but *more or less valid,* or valid for some purposes but not others. Notice that the most important issue is *what* is being measured, the **construct**.[50] The most important issue regarding the quality of an assessment is **CONSTRUCT VALIDITY**. In this example, the construct that the test is intended to measure is science achievement. But in the scientist's case, what the test actually measured was his achievement in English, a **rival construct** that **confounded** the validity of the inference of science achievement that could be drawn from his test score.

As these definitions and examples imply, validity cannot be proven.[51] But evidence of validity can be collected, and it may be possible to offer an argument that an assessment supports *substantially valid* inferences and uses. Some validity evidence is *theoretical*—for example, an expert's testimony that the science test's items represent the important content and principles in science. Such testimony would support an argument of **CONTENT VALIDITY**, of the test's relevance to and representativeness of the domain of science.[52] Such evidence is not proof. Controversy often exists in science as to what the field's important content and principles are, complicating an argument for content validity. Still, evidence of content validity contributes to an argument for construct validity, that the test really is measuring the construct science achievement, as intended. Construct validity subsumes content validity.

Some validity evidence is *empirical*—for example, test scores that are high for those test-takers who, like Pat, have a record of strong achievement in science and that are low for those test-takers who have a record of poor achievement in science offer evidence of the validity of inferences of achievement suggested by any of the compared tests. Comparing test scores to other performance indicators (i.e., **criterion measures**) of the same construct, such as other tests of science achievement or grade point averages (GPAs) in science classes, would support an argument of **CRITERION-RELATED VALIDITY**. Again, such evidence is not proof. The criterion measures might not represent the construct very well. For instance, the low scorers might have records of poor achievement in science not because they don't understand science but because their schools have poorly trained teachers and little science equipment, complicating an argument for criterion-related validity. Still, evidence of criterion-related validity contributes to an argument for construct validity, that the test really is measuring the construct science achievement, as claimed. Construct validity also subsumes criterion-related validity.

Even small changes in the learning context or the testing situation can have an impact on a student's scores and can change what is actually being measured—the construct. For example, imagine a math test administered following PE when Pat was too tired to pay attention, although she understood basic concepts. Or that she tended to get tired during the school day and could perform better on the same test in the morning than she could in the afternoon. Variations in students' motivation, interests, nutrition, distractibility, and innumerable other factors affect scores. So a score is partly a measure of the student's achievement related to the intended construct and partly a measure of such extraneous things (**rival**

constructs) as test anxiety and fatigue. For nearly all paper-and-pencil tests such as multiple-choice tests, reading ability is one test construct, intended or not.

Construct, content, and criterion-related validity are well-established principles in educational measurement.[53] Construct validity is the overarching principle, which subsumes both content validity and criterion-related validity. It subsumes newer conceptions of validity as well. The most important new validity concept is that of **CONSEQUENTIAL VALIDITY.**[54] In the definition of validity quoted earlier, reference was made to "the *adequacy* and *appropriateness* of *inferences* and *actions* based on test scores or other modes of assessment."[55] Consequential validity particularly highlights test-based actions.[56]

For example, as a consequence of college entrance exam scores, students every year are accepted to or excluded from colleges and universities. This is an example of high-stakes testing, the consequences of which are visited upon students, college hopefuls. The consequential validity question is: Are the decisions made regarding who is accepted and who is excluded valid? That is, are the students who are accepted able to meet college expectations and requirements? And are the applicants who are excluded unable to do the necessary work and spared the loss of time, energy, money, and self-esteem they might otherwise expend needlessly trying? Denial of admittance is a *negative consequence* but not an issue of consequential validity unless those accepted cannot meet the requirements (**false positives**) and/or those rejected could meet the requirements but are not given a chance (**false negatives**).

In this example of *consequences to students,* is the use of entrance exam scores to select students for college valid? If entrance exam scores were the only data considered in acceptance decisions, consequential validity might be a problem. It is widely known that college performance tends to be better predicted by high school GPAs than by college entrance exam scores (an issue of **PREDICTIVE VALIDITY**, one type of criterion-related validity, with college performance here serving as the criterion measure). Fewer false positives and false negatives might be expected when both entrance exam scores and GPAs are considered in acceptance decisions because use of **multiple assessment methods** tends to improve the validity of inferences and actions by giving more information about achievement than any single indicator would give.

However, although multiple assessment methods help, they do not guarantee valid inferences or actions. Imagine a returning student who, unmotivated in high school, earned a low GPA and low entrance exam scores but who is intellectually capable and now, years later, is willing to work hard. He or she is likely to be a false negative, capable of succeeding in college if given a chance but likely to be denied admittance based on early indicators that may well underestimate his or her college performance. And what of the charges that the tests yield lower scores for women, minorities, and the poor? Where the negative consequence of denial of admission falls disproportionately on identifiable groups, is there solid enough evidence that those who are accepted will really perform better than those who are rejected and that the tests are sparing members of these groups hopeless effort and inevitable failure? Do the tests exhibit **bias** against these groups, or do they adequately and appropriately sort future successes from would-be failures? These are questions of consequential validity, and they are subsumed under the fundamental construct validity question: What constructs are the tests really measuring? College aptitude? Or rival constructs such as motivation, gender, race, or socioeconomic status?

There may be consequences not only to students but also to teachers, schools, the curriculum, and pedagogy. An example of *consequences to teachers:* In the legal case of *St. Louis Teachers Union v. St. Louis Board of Education,* teachers who had been placed on probation because of their students' scores on the California Achievement Test (CAT) sued in 1985, because the teachers' property rights had been jeopardized as a consequence of this action of the board of education. Essentially, the teachers challenged the validity of the action of placing them on probation. After a two-year legal struggle, this use of test scores was overturned by the courts. In validity language, the inference drawn from the scores (and embodied in the probationary action) that the teachers had not done a good enough job of teaching was not deemed adequate and appropriate and was not considered valid.

An example of *consequences to schools:* Interview data from a 1998 study of local administration of state-mandated performance assessments included the following statement from a high school principal in Michigan. (At the time of the study, scores on the state's High School Proficiency Test, which included performance items, did not result in high stakes to students such as denial of graduation, and parents could write letters to have their children excused from taking the test.)

We have some parent exemptions. Either the parents are making a political statement, or they just don't want to be bothered. As a parent, I'd struggle with why—"Why should Maggie take the test?" I think it's a good test, and kids should want to show what they can do, but this test has no meaning. I'm not anticipating good results this year because of the lack of high stakes. There's just no reason for the kids to do well. If a few blow it off, statistically you're dead. I'm anticipating a big disaster.

Very capable kids tend to be the ones who are exempt, so the school results are naturally skewed to the lower end. We get criticized for it. It's frustrating. In the press, individual differences don't matter, don't get reported. The charts and graphs, the numbers are what people look at. If I try to explain the scores, the public will think it's an excuse. They'll just look at the numbers—

"Numbers don't lie." I'm hoping the neighboring districts will have more exemptions than we do. It's bizarre.[57]

This principal was worried that his school would suffer public humiliation and loss of local confidence because of an invalid inference based on test scores that the school was doing a poor job of education.

An example of *curricular consequences:* In a 15-month study of two schools in Arizona in which the widely used Iowa Test of Basic Skills (ITBS) was administered, it was found that teachers began to alter their curricula in favor of the content of the test even when they realized that "teaching to the test" degraded the educational opportunity of their students. They prioritized those subjects that were tested and neglected those that were not tested until, finally, "social studies and health instruction disappeared altogether."[58] For reading and math, subjects which were both tested and taught, the topics prominent on the test began to dominate the curriculum as

teachers tended to slight topics within math and reading that the test does not cover. For example, the sixth grade . . . skipped over metrics and pre-algebra to stress geometry skills on the basis of teachers' memory of what the math test covers. They never quite got back to the neglected topics or treated them with much less intensity.[59]

Teachers experienced feelings of "alienation and dissonance," "anxiety and guilt."[60] Those who did not succumb to the pressure to distort their curricula

pay a price for their resistance. They are likely to be subject to frequent demands to defend their programs on other grounds, and to fears that they will suffer sanctions and loss of autonomy.[61]

An example of *pedagogical consequences:* The same study also found that, as test pressure mounted, at one elementary school, there was

time set aside daily for the pupils to work on exercises that would improve their skills of grammar, punctuation, capitalization, spelling, and usage (the subtests of the ITBS language test). It was clear that these exercises would have formats similar to ITBS items.[62]

As the teaching methods began to mirror the format of ITBS test items, researchers concluded that "multiple-choice testing leads to multiple-choice teaching. . . . Over time and with increased testing stakes, teaching becomes more testlike."[63]

Specific test preparation of this type is becoming increasingly common[64] and raises questions about the appropriateness of the curricular and pedagogical consequences of testing and the deprofessionalization of teachers, questions of consequential validity. But instead of attributing the problem to testing, the public tends to "hold accountable" low-performing students or their teachers, a case of blaming the victims, and to continue to increase the pressure, which magnifies the problem. For example,

> A tough new policy that ties grade promotion exclusively to scores on a state standardized test has spurred stark gains in student performance, school officials in Waco, Texas say.
>
> The first policy of its kind in the state, the Waco policy demands that students in third through eighth grades get a combined passing grade on the reading and math portions of the Texas Assessment of Academic Skills (TAAS) or repeat a grade. First and second graders must pass the Iowa Test of Basic Skills.
>
> While nearly a third of almost 10,000 student in first through eighth grades were expected to be held back in Waco schools—where nearly 80 percent of students qualify for free- or reduced-price lunch—school officials now project only 20 percent will be forced to repeat a grade.
>
> Says Superintendent Rosanne Stripling, "We've definitely made some big strides." Officials attribute gains of about 10 percentage points in nearly every grade to better teaching methods and the prospect of a humiliating retention for students and parents.[65]

The humiliation is clear. The "better teaching methods" are undescribed. Richard Valencia, a testing and educational psychology professor at the University of Texas warned, "What they are doing in Waco is not a good idea. We have to keep in mind that these children are in their very formative stages of learning. This will damage their self-esteem."[66] Waco parents filed legal suit, claiming that the test was never intended to support retention decisions (a validity issue), but the suit was dismissed in district court.[67] Their attorney, Michael B. Roberts, claimed, "The TAAS tests show a disparate impact on Hispanic and black students that raises questions of equal protection and equality of the law."[68]

Other new validity ideas and subconcepts also direct attention to the relationship of testing to learning opportunities and environments. These include[69]

- **SYSTEMIC VALIDITY:**[70] The resonance between the test and the educational system, a subconcept of consequential validity referring to the consequences of testing to the system such as changes in curriculum and pedagogy and school organization. Where test-related actions support or improve the system, positive consequences offer evidence of systemic validity. Where test-related actions undermine or deform the system, negative consequences offer evidence of systemic invalidity.

- **INSTRUCTIONAL VALIDITY:** The resonance between the test and the curriculum and pedagogy experienced by the test-taker. As before, where test-related actions support or improve instruction, positive consequences offer evidence of instructional validity and vice versa.

- **ECOLOGICAL VALIDITY:** The resonance between the test environment and the learning environment. If the testing environment is similar to the environment in which learning or application occurs, the test-taker is likely to perform on the test similarly to the way he or she performs in the natural performance setting; test performance is likely to reflect the test-taker's actual knowledge and skills and vice versa.

Validity and the Personalized Assessment Paradigm

Consider the accumulation of validity concerns sketched above: concerns about test bias, concerns about denial of college admittance on the basis of test scores, concerns about jeopardizing teachers' jobs on the basis of test scores, concerns about narrowing of curricula, concerns about developmentally and sequentially inappropriate pedagogy, concerns about public misunderstanding and school humiliation, concerns about draconian test-based student retention policy.[71] Is it a coincidence that these validity challenges all emerged from standardized testing? Could we achieve better validity if we personalized rather than standardized assessment?

My claim is that personalized assessment tends to promote more valid inferences of the achievement of individuals than does standardized testing. This is because customized, concentrated focus on individuals provides a more complete portrait of individual achievement, especially when using a variety of measures over time. It's simple: Valid inferences of the achievement of an individual are enhanced by focus on the individual. This offers a strong psychometric argument in favor of a new approach to assessment.

Personalized assessment tends to be expansionist in nature, often involving the collection of an array of evidence of achievement: the aforementioned multiple methods and sources, which tend to improve the validity of inferences. Personalized assessment also tends to be expansionist in keeping open evaluative thinking, protecting the space for consideration and reconsideration, encouraging deeper analysis of assessment data by not prematurely offering a summative, door-closing, final judgment in the form of a score or grade. A body of evidence of achievement, rather than just a score, takes some time to understand. This is both blessing and curse—a promotion of more valid inferences at the expense of efficiency.

In addition to the threat to efficiency, personalized assessment invites a danger to reliability: Are assessors more likely to disagree when they are presented with a body of achievement evidence, an array likely to include some degree of ambiguity and contradiction? Are they more likely to summon different criteria and standards for different pieces and from different assessors? Are elaboration and disagreement natural, healthy, productive—or psychometrically intolerable?

Reliability is an important issue both theoretically and practically. In practice, the failure of Kentucky's state-mandated performance assessments to post sufficient interrater reliability, in the view of evaluators, was the primary reason the state lost its performance assessment system.[72] Charges of unreliability also raised concern about Vermont's portfolio system[73] and about Pittsburgh's widely admired Arts Propel portfolios,[74] no longer thriving as a district practice. Clearly, reliability needs careful consideration.

Reliability

Reliability refers to the consistency of scores. For standardized multiple-choice tests, reliability has typically been conceptualized as the replication of scores on the same or an equivalent or parallel form of a test. If Pat performs at about the same level time after time on the same test (or equivalent forms of the same test), the scores are said to be reliable and the test is said to produce reliable scores.[75] This is the basic idea, although reliability is calculated for groups of test-takers rather than individuals.

Another way to think about reliability is to consider the relationship between *true score*, the highest score of which a test-taker is truly capable, and *observed scores*, the scores the test-taker actually posts. The actual scores include *measurement error*, making them either higher or lower than the unknowable true score. Actual scores that are unreliable or inconsistent are typically interpreted as including a lot of measurement error, the error considered to be the reason for the differences. Actual scores that are reliable or consistent are typically interpreted as converging on—not necessarily pinpointing—the true score. If it could be detected, the true score would provide the best basis for valid inferences of achievement. Because true score can only be inferred, consistent actual scores are considered a better basis for valid inferences than are inconsistent actual scores.

Often, however, the reliability of standardized multiple-choice tests is not investigated. Instead, claims of reliability are based on internal consistency procedures,[76] which determine how well performance on each item in a test predicts the overall score. That is, the most frequently used mathematical formulas calculate the correlation between good performance on each test item with good performance on the test as a whole. It is easier to determine internal consistency because it requires the test to be administered only once to a population of test-takers, whereas replicability of performance requires the test (or equivalent forms of a test) to be administered repeatedly. But internal consistency is not reliability. And there is less reason to believe that a test's internal consistency supports valid inferences of achievement, because similarity of items might misrepresent a domain that is complex and various.[77]

For performance assessments, test-takers are usually not asked to replicate their performances. These performances take more time than multiple-choice test items, limiting opportunity and the feasibility of retakes. Also, because the assessments themselves are often educative, the first experience of a performance task is more likely to affect and improve the second performance. For performance assessments, reliability typically refers to agreement among different raters about the score for a single performance. That is, do the assessors agree that Pat's performance rates an A? If they agree, there is interrater reliability. **INTERRATER RELIABILITY** refers to consistent scores awarded by different assessors for the same performance.

An example of *interrater reliability:* If a panel of judges scores science fair projects and all agree that Pat's project should win the blue ribbon, their assessments exhibit interrater reliability. If one judge disagrees, his score would be considered unreliable. In some situations, unreliable scores are discarded. For instance, in some Olympics performances, the highest score and the lowest score from a panel of judges are thrown out. In educational performance assessments, raters whose scores differ from those of other raters are typically retrained or dismissed.

Agreement, consistency, and reliability are important where assessments convey high stakes. It would be intolerable—and legally provocative—to deny a senior a diploma if the assessors could not agree whether her performance on a high school exit examination was sufficient for graduation, or to retain a first grader if his score on the state achievement test was failing on Monday but passing on Tuesday. Consistency gives confidence that important decisions are right. The problem is that it is possible for scores to be consistent but wrong, as when the renowned scientist consistently scores a zero on a science test written in a language he cannot understand—an instance of reliability without validity. It is also possible for assessors to agree but to be wrong—a fallibility of consensus. Reliability is important for confidence but not sufficient for validity.

The Relationship Between Validity and Reliability

It is dogma in the field of measurement that reliability is necessary but not sufficient for validity.[78] That is, a test cannot support valid inferences unless it is also reliable—one cannot infer that Pat is good at science if she makes a high score on the test one day and a low score on an equivalent form of the test the next day, or that the figure skater deserves the gold medal if half the judges don't think so. But a test can produce reliable scores without supporting valid inferences—the South American scientist will get a low score every time he takes the test in English, but inferences that he is ignorant of science will be invalid.

All that is needed for reliability is consistent scores. Reliability does not mean one can rely on a test to do what it is intended to do. Validity, the more important quality, is not so easily shown. Test developers work hard to achieve high reliability. This is partly because a claim of test quality can be supported on the basis of the test's production of reliable scores, partly because a showing of reliability has been taken as support for a claim of validity. But what if the long-standing claim about the nature of the relationship between these two concepts were different? What if reliability was neither necessary nor sufficient for validity?

I have argued that reliability—although important for confidence—is unrelated to validity.[79] This lack of relationship is illustrated in a couple of simplistic examples. Regarding reliability, assume Pat takes a test (or equivalent forms of the test) on four different occasions. On three occasions, she is awarded a low score. Once, she is starting to contract the flu; another time, her parakeet has just died; the third time, she is sleep deprived after a late party; the fourth time, she in good mental and physical health. She scores well only on the fourth occasion. But this score is inconsistent with the three previous lower scores, unreliable by definition, and thrown out—although it is the only score that can support a valid inference of her achievement.[80]

Note the similarity to the celebrated case, *Peter Dalton v. Educational Testing Service* (1995), in which Brian Dalton's father sued the Educational Testing Service (ETS) for refusal to release the higher of Brian's two scores on the Scholastic Aptitude Test (SAT). Dalton claimed he had been ill on the first testing occasion, whereas ETS maintained that a difference in health was insufficient to explain the discrepancy between his two scores and that the SAT produced more reliable scores than Dalton's unless there was some interference. Dalton won.

Regarding interrater reliability, a similar scenario can be constructed in which all but one judge is ill, bored, distracted, or lacking the relevant expertise to evaluate a performance. Only the healthy, alert, expert judge awards a score—whether high or low—which could support valid inferences of the quality of the performance and the skill of the performer. Her score is discarded or she is dismissed because her score differs from that of the other judges—although it is the only score that can support a valid inference of the performer's achievement. This hypothetical scenario and that of Pat's are so easily imagined, it seems inevitable they must sometimes occur.

Because a score can support valid inferences of achievement even if it is not consistent with other scores, reliability is neither necessary nor sufficient for validity. Of course, reliability may support valid inferences of achievement, and it may be reasonable to presume it does in many cases, but reliability is not a prerequisite for validity. We want reliability because we will have more confidence that Pat's science fair project is the best if all the judges agree that it is than if only half the judges think so.

Like standardized test developers, most performance assessment developers also seek reliability as evidence of the quality of their assessment systems. This is especially true for large-scale and high-stakes assessments. But it has proven harder to achieve reliability with performance assessments. Reliability problems cause anguish[81] and have sometimes contributed to the revision or abandonment of performance assessment systems.

Experience has led to common realization that certain features of a performance assessment system tend to improve interrater reliability:

- Performance standards or rubrics that direct all assessors to look for the same aspects and qualities in student papers or performances

- Performance criteria about which all assessors are likely to agree (simple criteria such as, in writing, "usage/mechanics/grammar" rather than complex criteria such as "persuasiveness" or "significance of theme" or "effective use of figurative language" are more likely to yield reliability)

- Short measurement scales, typically 3 to 6 measurement points or standards, which limit the possible diversity in scores

- Arbitrarily defining unreliability in such a way as to render it improbable (e.g., Vermont's stipulated definition of unreliability required scores that differed by 2 or more measurement points. This meant that reliability was not compromised if one Vermont rater identified purpose *frequently* in a paper and another identified purpose *sometimes*. This limited the possibility of unreliable scores to three combinations that appear unlikely: *extensively* and *sometimes, frequently* and *rarely,* and *extensively* and *rarely.*)

- Training raters to score similarly and retraining or dismissing those who differ

These features contribute to reliable scores, but do they enhance validity or contribute to assessment quality? I believe that "rigging the system"[82] to get reliability comes at the expense of validity. For example, use of simplistic criteria obstructs recognition of sophisticated performance. Short measurement scales prevent fine distinctions that might better reflect performance quality. The fewer the measurement points or performance standards or levels, the fewer miscategorizations of student work but the greater the loss of information about the meaning of the score[83] and the more serious any scoring errors,[84] painful if high stakes are triggered by a minimum performance level or cut-score. Adjustments to improve reliability, the very feature believed to demonstrate the psychometric quality of a performance assessment system and undeniably important, also unintentionally undermines quality by compromising validity, the most important psychometric property.

Things like short measurement scales of 4 to 6 score points, stipulated definitions of reliability that are unlikely to be often met in practice, training assessors for lock-step consensus in scoring, and simplistic scoring criteria about which raters can agree and avoidance of complex criteria about which they are less likely to agree do tend to improve interrater reliability, but they do so artificially and they obstruct validity. Reliability is needed, and it should be monitored. But direct moves to strengthen reliability, such as these, undermine validity. Because validity is the goal, strengthening reliability at the expense of validity is counterproductive. This is why it is important to understand that reliability is not a prerequisite for validity, that there is tension between the two concepts, and that reliability may suggest validity but does not contribute to it. *Naturally occurring reliability,*[85] rather than artificially enhanced reliability, is helpful. Moves to improve assessments should be aimed more at validity, less at reliability.

Performance assessment systems are perverted when techniques that encourage students to demonstrate complex and unique achievement are subjected to scoring methods that discourage complex and unique performance. Performance assessment systems are damaged by standardization because the opportunity to learn about the achievement of the student is restricted or lost. Performance assessment systems are compromised when emphasis on reliability encourages standardization that deflects attention away from the student.

A Personal Position

My argument that personalized assessment supports more valid inferences of individual student achievement than does standardized assessment is based on recognition of the importance of directing attention to the student whose achievement is being assessed, considering a variety of forms of evidence of achievement, and attending to the complexity and uniqueness of achievement the student demonstrates. This argument is also based on the premise that inferences will be more valid and assessments more equitable if assessors consider rival constructs and relevant factors affecting performance, if their judgments take into account the student's learning opportunity, academic history, personal circumstances, interests, and goals. We can make more valid inferences about a student's achievement from assessments that are relevant to what the student has had the opportunity and interest to learn and that allow the student some input in determining the appropriate time and means of expressing that. The development of valid inferences of a student's achievement requires complex judgment about complex evidence, not simplistic criteria, as well as flexibility and willingness to consider the student's ideas and characteristics, not rigid external scoring procedures. This argument is also based on recognition that all assessment judgments, instruments, and processes are subjective—even so-called objective tests, which, in fact, merely offer machine-scorable selected-response items rather than human-scorable constructed-response items. Even in the most standardized tests and assessments, humans make many subjective judgments in constructing the test and determining what will count as relevant knowledge and correct answers, developing and implementing administration protocols, and programming the machine. All assessment is subjective.

This is not the general view in the measurement community, especially traditionalists who see their responsibility as centered in group scores and comparisons mostly for predictive purposes, who believe that bias can be minimized by standards and criteria and rubrics, or who insist that equity requires treating students identically no matter how diverse they and their circumstances actually are. Formal criteria and standards, rubrics, and the press for reliability all tend toward standardization, to work against individualization.

The same standardization that promotes reliability also yields test results that are not very reflective of the complexities of what a student has learned, too sketchy to get a very complete view of what a student knows and can do. Attention to rubrics and criteria diverts attention from individual performance and obstructs understanding the achievement of a student. Rather than promoting validity, the reductive scores from standardized assessments and from prespecified, simplistic rubrics ignore the actual complexity of the student's achievement. External referents, such as normative comparisons and prespecified criteria, help by locating performance. But rather than promoting education, they offer very little feedback that might help teachers understand student learning or provide optimal curricula and learning conditions.

Reporting Assessment Results

Feedback and reporting of assessment results can be accomplished in different ways, particularly, measurement scales or narrative feedback and reporting.

The advantages and disadvantages of grading or scoring in contrast to narrative assessment are not well recognized. Most people are not well acquainted with formal narrative assessment and are so familiar with grading that they cannot quite imagine an alternative. Narrative reporting provides students and teachers with much more feedback, feedback that helps to develop a deep understanding of students' achievements. Most teachers must, of course, give grades, but that doesn't preclude narrative assessment as well.

What grading or scoring can provide:

- a summative indicator of how much the student has learned;
- a summative indicator of how well the student has performed;
- if there is a cut-score, whether or not the student performed well enough;
- if scores are norm referenced or if grading on a curve, an indicator of the student's performance relative to other students or a norming sample;
- if scores are criterion referenced, how well the student performed in terms of predetermined criteria;
- if scores are standards based, how well the student performed in terms of prespecified standards; and
- a referent, a basis for comparison to criteria, standards, and/or other test-takers.

What narrative reporting can provide:

- assessors' judgments of how much the student has learned;
- assessors' judgments of how well the student performed;
- assessors' judgments of whether or not the student performed well enough;
- assessors' judgments of whether the student met criteria and standards, if these have been formalized, and how they were applied;
- formative or summative information detailing specifics of the quality of the student's performance, including strengths and weaknesses;
- assessors' explanations or rationales for their judgments; and
- suggestions for future work.

It is true that narrative assessment can be subverted, reduced to "nice job" comments that convey no more information than a grade or score, circumventing the potential benefits of customized critique. Still, narrative assessment provides an opportunity for educative feedback. It is not necessarily a choice between a grade or a narrative commentary; a combination might be selected. Grading or scoring can accompany rather than supplant narrative feedback or vice versa. The point here is to recognize the possibility for fullness and detail in narrative reporting, not just

A–

on an assignment to produce a critical annotated bibliography, for example, but

> Your summaries and critical review of the journal articles you annotated for this assignment show good sensitivity to theoretical and ethical issues. A particular strength was your juxtaposition of the authors' assumptions and interpretations of their data with various conceptual explanations of what it means for a student to be "at-risk" and whether the locus of the problem is in the student, the student's personal surround, or the system. I was impressed that you considered not only methodological ethics (e.g., anonymity of students, direct and indirect observer effects on students) but also the ethical implications of theoretical assumptions (e.g., effects on self-esteem of thinking of at-riskness as a deficit in students, characterizing them as inadequate rather than the system's response to them as inadequate). However, the questions you formulated for future research based on this literature were little more than restatements of the research questions in these articles, not very productive for advancing the field. See if you can give more thought to what is missing in the literature, if that suggests how your research might pick up where these articles leave off.

Narrative feedback of this type is not less evaluative, not less rigorous, not less specific about the basis for the judgment made about the student's performance than the grade was, and it is much more useful than the grade. The benefit is to both the student, who has a much better idea of what worked well, how well, and why and to the teacher,[86] who pondered what worked well, how well, and why—and in the process improved her understanding of the student's achievement, articulated the basis for the assessment, and gained a better sense of how to develop and revise curriculum as a result.

Notes

1. Where about two thirds of all measures will fall within 1 standard deviation, plus or minus, of the average and about 95% of all measures will fall within 2 standard deviations, plus or minus, of the average.

2. Determining standard scores is more complicated than simply calculating an average and comparing each student's raw score to the average, although this simplified explanation does convey the basic strategy. Standard scores actually involve calculating the standard deviation of a distribution of scores and using the standard deviation to locate each raw score on one of several standard scales (e.g., percentiles, stanines, grade-equivalent scores). The location of a raw score on the scale is the standard score. Using the normal curve as the scale forces the actual distribution of scores into a normal distribution.

3. Vermont Department of Education (1991). Vermont has changed to a New Standards Project format (E. Grainger, personal communication, September 8, 1998).

4. See traditional measurement textbooks such as Gronlund (1993) and nontraditional performance assessment guides such as Illinois State Board of Education (1995).

5. Adapted from Calandra (1968).

6. Sharing criteria in advance with students is recommended by proponents of all three paradigms. See, for example, Gronlund (1993, psychometric paradigm); Cole, Ryan, and Kick (1995, contextual paradigm); and Wiggins (1993, personalized paradigm).

7. Mabry (1999) and Mabry, Daytner, and Aldarondo (1999).

8. See Hillocks (1997) for an empirical study of performance assessment, which found that, in Illinois, use of rubrics for scoring had the effect of standardizing student writing.

9. Bloom, Englehart, Furst, Hill, and Krathwohl (1956).

10. Daugherty (1995, p. 119).

11. The classic five-paragraph theme includes a first paragraph, which states the topic or thesis and previews points of support, which will be the subjects of the next three paragraphs, then ends with a final summary paragraph.

12. Hillocks (1997).

13. Definition adapted from Linn (1994).

14. Definition adapted from GOALS 2000 (1994).

15. Definition adapted from GOALS 2000 (1994).

16. Mabry (1997b).

17. Lazarovici (1997).

18. Porter (1995).

19. National Council of Teachers of Mathematics (1989).

20. Collins (1997) and Mabry, Daytner, and Aldarondo (1999).

21. Among those who have questioned specification of same standards for all is Eisner (1992).

22. Among those who have worried about testing that hurts students with inferior learning opportunities is Darling-Hammond (1994).

23. Ipsative assessments that feature forced-choice formats, such as Kuder's Vocational Preference Record, raise a validity problem in that a choice on one dimension precludes a choice on another dimension. Thus, a test-taker's true scores might be high in two dimensions but his or her observed scores would not (Aiken, 1989, pp. 280-281). This is not a problem in performance assessments that feature constructed-response rather than forced-choice items.

24. Source: Rhode Island State Assessment Program (1996).

25. Source: Wisconsin Department of Public Instruction (1995-1996).

26. See Gitomer (1993) for a discussion of authenticity and ill-defined problems.

27. For more discussion, see Mabry (1995a) and Wiggins (1993).

28. Schön (1995).

29. Standardization of writing has been reported as occurring in Illinois as a result of use of rubrics; misscoring of the type described here has been reported as occurring in Texas with state-mandated direct writing assessments (see Hillocks, 1997). See also Mabry (1999).

30. As described in Gitomer (1993) and Raven (1992).

31. Such decisions are documented in observations of CTB/McGraw-Hill's trained scorers in California (Colvin, 1997).

32. Some such studies are Mabry (1995c, 1997b) and Mabry and Daytner (1997).

33. For critical analysis of these assumptions, see Berlak (1992a), Berliner and Biddle (1995), and Resnick and Resnick (1992).

34. Mabry (in preparation-a).

35. Mabry and Daytner (1997).

36. Mabry (1995c) and Part 2, this volume.

37. With Melody Shank, I visited the school in Spring 1995, informally observing and talking with faculty, administrators, and students.

38. Haladyna, Nolen, and Haas (1991).

39. See, for example, American Educational Research Association, American Psychological Association, and the National Council on Measurement in Education's (AERA, APA, NCME; 1998) *Standards for Educational and Psychological Testing*, and Conoly and Impara's (1995) *The Twelfth Mental Measurements Yearbook* (see also other *Mental Measurements Yearbooks* by the Buros Institute, 12 editions).

40. See http://www.waco.isd.tenet.edu/focus.html (June 12, 1998).

41. The 90% mark is also the state's determiner for an "exemplary" school rating; see http://www.teachermagazine.org/sreports/qc98/solutions/so-s2.htm (June 13, 1998).

42. Brooks (1998a).

43. "Texas School" (1998).

44. See http://www.teachermagazine.org/sreports/qc98/solutions/so-s2. htm.

45. Gonzalez (1998), Mabry (1997c), and Mabry and Gonzalez (in preparation).

46. See http://www.teachermagazine.org/sreports/qc98/solutions/so-s2.html.

47. For a fuller argument, see Mabry (1995c).

48. AERA, APA, NCME (1998, Chapter 1, p. 1).

49. Messick (1989, p. 13, emphasis in the original).

50. Measurement concepts are evolving. An emerging definition of construct from the March 23, 1998 draft of the *Standards for Educational and Psychological Testing* (AERA, APA, NCME, 1998) refers to "the construct or concepts the test is intended to measure. Examples of constructs include mathematics achievement, performance as a computer technician, depression, or self-esteem" (Chapter 1, p. 1). "As used here, a construct is evoked whenever meaning is attached to a test score or to a pattern of test responses. This is in sharp contrast to some historical uses of the term, which reserve the term 'construct' for characteristics that are not directly observable, but which are inferred from interrelated sets of observations" (Introduction, p. 5). For an earlier definition and discussion of constructs, see Cronbach and Meehl (1955).

51. See Cole (1988), Cronbach (1988), and Messick (1989).

52. The defining characteristics of content validity are the test content's representativeness of and relevance to the domain of the construct (Messick, 1989).

53. AERA, APA, NCME (1985, 1998). *Face validity*, not mentioned in the text here and not usually considered a technical subcategory of validity, refers to the obviousness of the construct in the test, whether—on the face of it, at a glance, or to a lay audience—it appears that the test will measure the construct intended.

54. Messick (1975, 1989), see also Linn, Baker, and Dunbar (1991) and Moss (1992).

55. Messick (1989, p. 13, emphasis in the original).

56. It is occasionally claimed that consequential validity is not really a type or issue of validity at all and that test consequences (or some test consequences) are unrelated to validity. But validity is a property of inferences and uses and, in fact, the inferences are often apparent because they are embodied in the uses of test scores in educational decision making and reporting. Actions based on scores—uses—are consequences. There are often unintended consequences of test use as well. About this matter, there are careful statements in the latest draft of *Standards for Educational and Psychological Testing* (AERA, APA, NCME, 1998): "It is important to distinguish between evidence that is directly relevant to validity and evidence that may inform decisions about social policy but falls outside the realm of validity" (Chapter 1, p. 11). "Although information about the consequences of testing may influence decisions about test use, such consequences do not in and of themselves detract from the validity of intended test interpretations. . . . Thus, evidence about consequences may be directly relevant to validity when it can be traced to a source of invalidity such as construct underrepresentation or construct irrelevant components" (Chapter 1, p. 12).

57. Anonymous Michigan principal, personal communication, April 29, 1998.

58. Smith (1991, p. 10).

59. Smith (1991, p. 9).

60. Smith (1991, p. 10).

61. Smith (1991, p. 10).

62. Smith (1991, p. 10).

63. Smith (1991, p. 10).

64. See, for example, Hillocks (1997); Mabry (1997c, pp. 17-18); anonymous Chicago teacher, personal communication, March 19, 1998.

65. "Texas School" (1998).

66. Brooks (1998b).

67. Lemire (1998). One suing parent was a former school board president.

68. Brooks (1998a). *Disparate impact* is one legal standard by which the courts might rule against test use (see Phillips, 1993).

69. See also Lather (1986), on *catalytic validity* in qualitative research.

70. Frederiksen and Collins (1989).

71. See also "Sixty Years" (1987).

72. R. K. Hill, personal communication, April 17, 1998. See Hambleton et al. (1995).

73. Koretz (1992) and Koretz, Stecher, Klein, and McCaffrey (1994).

74. Camp (1990), LeMahieu (1993), Rothman (1992), and Wolf, Bixby, Glenn, and Gardner (1991).

75. This presumes Pat's achievement level is unchanged between testing sessions (e.g., she doesn't learn a lot more science between taking Form A and

Form B, doesn't learn enough about the test from Form A to raise her score on Form B).

76. For example, Kuder-Richardson formula 20 and Kuder-Richardson formula 21.

77. Ennis (1980) observed: "The heavily used indices of reliability, the Kuder-Richardson formulas, are indices of *the extent to which every item correlates with every other item on a single administration of the test.* The more homogeneous the items the higher this coefficient of internal consistency" (p. 24, emphasis in the original). The problem is that many domains are not homogeneous.

78. See any standard measurement textbook, for example, Gronlund (1993), Hopkins, Stanley, and Hopkins (1990), Kubiszyn and Borich (1996), and Worthen, Borg, and White (1993).

79. Mabry (1995a).

80. Pat might also perform above her actual achievement level for a variety of reasons, leading to erroneously inflated inferences of her achievement.

81. For example, the RAND report of Vermont's portfolio system reported low reliability as a serious counterindicator of assessment quality (Koretz, 1992, 1993; Koretz et al., 1994), and Arts PROPEL portfolios in the Pittsburgh public schools were similarly criticized when teachers' ratings differed from others' (see LeMahieu, 1993; see also Camp, 1990; LeMahieu & Eresh, 1996; Rothman, 1992).

82. On one public occasion, a member of the Vermont Department of Education so described the state's short, 4-point measurement scale and the stipulated definition of interrater unreliability (Brewer, 1991, in response to questions).

83. Yen (1997).

84. Linn (1997).

85. Mabry (1995a) and Moss (1994).

86. In this case, myself. These are my comments today to a student in my Introduction to Research Methods class on an assignment to produce a critical annotated bibliography and research questions informed by the reviewed literature. The comments accompanied a grade of A−.

FIVE

Equity

Context heavily influences the equity implications of different approaches to assessment.[1] Normative strategies and the standardization they have engendered, born in a more innocent age (or were we merely more naïve?), are fair only if students have equal access to good education. Our country has never achieved educational equity and is not likely to do so, as the scandalous record of disparities in school finance and the many cases of litigation against states for inequitable funding attest. Many believe that the privileged classes will never be compelled to equalize educational opportunities by redistributing some of the resources their children enjoy and that they will control policy for their own benefit or, where they cannot, will find loopholes. This implacability is demonstrated, for example, in the "civil war" of the affluent against the 1998 Vermont Act 60 legislation to equalize school funding.[2] Educational, economic, and social privileges are safeguarded partly by tests that are taken as proof of the superior capabilities of middle- and upper-class children.

The intractable unfairness in educational opportunity has figured in the move toward national assessment as discussion has fluctuated from assessment to achievement standards to delivery standards intended to ensure that all schools deliver high-quality education before students are held accountable. In the ongoing debate around the ubiquitous phrase "high standards for all," proponents of such standards tend to argue that all students should be held to the same standards and tend to favor standardized assessments (sometimes standardized performance assessments). Others maintain that high standards for all are inequitable nonsense when not all children have equal opportunity to learn. No one argues against the need to improve the quality of education or against high standards. But holding all students to the same standards, given the inequities in the system, punishes low-scoring students for circumstances that, for a great many, are beyond their control—circumstances that negatively affect test scores and that are on the rise.[3] In addition, judging all students by the same standards, given the natural diversity of human beings, also denies individuality and forces compliance and uniformity,[4] another kind of human injustice, however inadvertent.

The assessment paradigms suggest dramatically different views of equity. The personalized paradigm assumes the only way to be fair is to recognize the uniqueness of student interests, achievements, goals, and circumstances. How else can you give each student a fair hearing? The psychometric paradigm assumes the only way to be fair is to give students identical, secure tests under identical conditions. How else can you compare student performance impartially? The difficulty with personalization from a traditional point of view is suggested in an agonized analysis of a testing situation in which a very limited amount of choice was permitted to students:

> In the case of portfolio assessment, the element of choice is implicit and not amenable to many of the kinds of analysis that have been described here. . . . In portfolio assessment, how many forms of the test are created by examinee choice? Often, as many as there are examinees! If that is the case, can those forms be statistically equated? No. . . . [T]he reliability of the 1992 Vermont portfolio program measures was substantially less than is expected for useful measurement. Can it be otherwise, when the examinees (effectively) construct their own tests?
>
> Is building examinee choice into a test possible? Yes, but it requires extra work. Approaches that ignore the empirical possibility that different items do not have the same difficulty will not satisfy the canons of good testing practice, nor will they yield fair tests.
>
> What can we do if the assumptions required for equating are not satisfied across the choice items? If test forms are built that cannot be equated (made comparable), scores comparing individuals on incomparable forms have their validity compromised by the portion of the test that is not comparable. Thus, we cannot fairly allow choice if the process of choosing cannot be adjusted away.
>
> Choice is anathema to standardized testing unless those aspects that characterize the choice are irrelevant to what is being tested.[5]

The holding power of the old assumptions and methods is clear, the presumption that comparison is the right strategy for determining achievement, the necessity of standardization and equivalent test forms and items to facilitate comparison, the collapsing of the distinction between equity and comparability, and the difficulty of seeing beyond the familiar paradigmatic horizon.

No assessment paradigm or technique guarantees equity. Performance assessment might even widen the gap between haves and have-nots.[6] Still, standardized testing and the enforcement of identical standards for all impose sameness, not fairness. It is a mistake to confuse the two. It is a costly mistake because it suggests a rationale for raising the assessment bar to the same height for everyone without leveling the playing field. Children denied good education must jump higher to clear the bar because they jump from lower ground. It is doubly unjust—the denial of good education followed by the imposition of identical standards. Standardized testing has helped to generate the overwhelming empirical evidence that nurtured children succeed and neglected children fail and has helped to align educational measurement with social reproduction. This alignment is particularly onerous because education is our society's prime vehicle for opposing social reproduction and for promoting individual self-improvement and social meritocracy. In this way, standardized assessment opposes education and equity.

Equity cannot be guaranteed by methodological fiat, but fairness *may* be enhanced—not necessarily *will* be enhanced—if assessment is personalized, individualized enough to take into account the real differences among real children and their real opportunities. An important advantage of ipsative measures and individualized standards is that they allow opportunity to take into account relevant qualifiers, rival constructs that affect scores. These constructs cannot be edited out of assessment, but they need not overwhelm the validity or equity of our assessment-based inferences and actions.

I am not arguing against any and all uses of standardized testing or for any and all uses of performance assessment. Inferences of student achievement are enhanced when we have both good, detailed information about a child and also good reference points for locating his or her work among common expectations and general performance. I am arguing that we need more detail to understand the child and his or her idiosyncratic achievements, to fashion child-sensitive educational arrangements, to recognize what he or she knows and might be ready to learn next, and to work in his or her zone of proximal development.[7] If we can do that, we will have developed truly educational assessment, to which we would be well advised to add a bit of locational information. It is a matter of purpose, grand purpose, educational purpose. It is a matter of revising our priorities regarding different types of assessment: more ipsative, student-sensitive assessment; more contextualized, curriculum-based assessment; less standardized, comparison-facilitating assessment.

It is also a matter of equity. It is not likely that delivery standards can be set and enforced such that educational delivery systems will be made equal.[8] If equitable assessment depends on equitable provision of education, then assessment will never be equitable. Standardization presumes equitable distribution of educational resources, which does not exist. Even if educational delivery could be equalized, the validity and equity of educational assessment would still be compromised so long as all children, in their glorious diversity, were tested on identical content and held to identical standards. Such sameness insinuates into schooling a demand for conformity discordant with constructivist learning theory and disruptive of individual self-actualization.[9]

Consider the flexibility of the five teacher-developed assessment systems in Part 2, their responsiveness to curriculum and context and to individual students. Consider whether these assessment systems support valid inferences of student achievement, equity, teacher professionalism, and good education.

Notes

1. Context heavily influences legal judgments regarding equity, too. For example, a history of racial segregation was the crucial consideration in the judicial decision in *Debra P. v. Turlington* (1983) that use of Florida's State Student Assessment Test, Part 2, a functional literacy test that the district court held to be adequate in terms of content and construct validity and not racially biased, had nevertheless violated African American students' 14th Amendment equal protection rights.

2. Edwards (1998). The virulence of opponents of Act 60 was suggested in the imprudent remark of one: "It makes me feel like someone is going to get shot" (p. 35).

3. Massell, Kirst, and Hoppe (1997).

4. See Eisner (1993).

5. Wainer and Thissen (1994, pp. 190-191).

6. See Darling-Hammond (1994).

7. Vygotsky (1978).

8. See Porter (1995).

9. Maslow (1970).

PART TWO

Examples of
Assessments

Five examples of systems featuring different techniques will be described to illustrate some of the options and variety in curriculum-based and personalized assessment. Three are highly personalized systems, unusual not only for that but also because they are high school assessment systems—individualization is generally easier to accomplish in elementary grades where self-contained classrooms increase teacher-student familiarity. Two draw from both the personalized and the contextual assessment paradigms, attentive to curricula but with structures that embed opportunities for personalization without evidence of paradigmatic conflict. All are systems in which assessment plans or activities support particular kinds of teaching and learning in particular contexts with particular student bodies, demonstrating the adaptiveness of nonstandardized assessment. In the three personalized high school programs, the assessments also provide an important (in two systems even the primary) impetus and means of learning itself. These are examples of truly educative assessments woven into curricula almost seamlessly.

The literacy portfolios planned in 1993-1994 as the first phase of a multitechnique assessment system at Emily Dickinson Elementary School in Redmond, Washington offer a school-based contrast to the large-scale writing portfolios of Vermont. This contrast will be noted to show how a new assessment technique (in this case, the technique is portfolios) can be located within any of the three paradigms and how paradigmatic assumptions and approaches can resonate with or undermine the advantages of that technique (in this case, the advantage is strong opportunity for ipsative understandings and feedback). The different purposes of the two systems, Vermont's standardized and Emily Dickinson's a combination of contextual and personalized strategies, yielded distinctive portfolio designs, activities, products, and assessment values.

Next, the assessment activities of the Lake View Education and Arts Partnership (LEAP) in Chicago will be described. LEAP, established in 1994 in four Chicago schools partnered with community and neighborhood arts organizations, involves elementary and high school teachers working with artists in collaborative development and team-teaching of curriculum units that integrate academics and the fine arts. Curriculum-based assessments are tailored to each multisession instructional unit and feature a variety rather than a single assessment technique in response to the particularities of the units.

At the high school level, three assessment systems will be described that were developed entirely by teachers to address the specific needs of their students. First implemented in 1971-1972, the Rite of Passage Experience (R.O.P.E.) at Walden III High School in Racine, Wisconsin engages seniors in a yearlong assessment process involving portfolios, research projects, and demonstrations of mastery, the latter of which will be particularly described. R.O.P.E. demonstrations, required in all academic subjects and in several additional areas, are a high-stakes assessment on which eligibility for graduation depends.

Similarly, students who enrolled in Eagle's Wing, a specialized unit of Hudson's Bay High School in Vancouver, Washington, from 1993 to 1997, were assessed in a variety of subject areas on the basis of personalized projects. The accumulation of credits earned primarily in these projects, with some credits also earned in classes, were the basis of eligibility for graduation.

Learning contracts developed at neighboring Pan Terra High School were the inspiration for Eagle's Wing projects. Pan Terra is, like Walden, a well-established alternative school and, like Eagle's Wing, offers individualized programs of study of which classes are a relatively small part of the plan for earning credits toward graduation. Pan Terra contracts, negotiated individually between teacher and student, are the vehicles for planning the learning experiences and for assessing the work of students.

Discussion of these systems will include narrative descriptions based on personal contact, noting features of the assessment programs and their contexts and purposes, as well as analysis of such characteristics as utility, benefits, rigor, psychometric properties, and difficulties. Note that all these systems, even the most well established, experience (or experienced) a common difficulty: local suspicion. These systems exist within hostile macro-assessment environments dominated by standardized testing (rather than curriculum-based or ipsative assessment) and accountability schemes based on comparison of simplistic indicators (rather than understanding of complex, interrelated comprehension of students and influences). Suspicion is less related to assessment quality than to underappreciation, especially at Walden, which has accumulated an outstanding record attesting to the validity of inferences of student achievement based on R.O.P.E. School personnel at each site found it necessary to expend time and energy explaining their systems and defending themselves. This suggests a difficulty likely to be experienced by others undertaking new paradigm assessment development, although less perhaps as performance assessment is becoming increasingly familiar. This difficulty also makes apparent the high degree of dedication and energy of the faculties and staffs of these schools. Commitment to practicing and continually improving good assessment is particularly characteristic of the two most mature of these five programs, those at Walden and Pan Terra High Schools.

Emily Dickinson's Literacy Portfolios

At Emily Dickinson Elementary School in Redmond, Washington, the faculty and staff undertook a thoroughgoing effort to understand and incorporate best-practice strategies in several areas. By 1993, the school had formulated its own student outcomes and devised its own report card; many classrooms housed multiage student populations; cooperative and inquiry-based learning were prevalent; and teachers shared significantly in exercising authority in and for the school. Not coincidentally, Emily Dickinson was arguably the most inclusive school in the state at a time when inclusion of children eligible for special services in regular classrooms was not common practice. Principal Jeff Newport and the Emily Dickinson faculty and staff were justifiably proud of their hard-won accomplishments, which they believed to be very much in the best interests of their students and community.

Recognizing that standardized tests were unlikely to detect the full range and quality of their educational outcomes, school personnel became interested in developing an alternative means to provide for both assessment of student achievement and school accountability.[1] In 1992-1993, they began in earnest to develop a system resonant with their educational methods and goals.

Design Considerations

In creating a school-based assessment system for Emily Dickinson's students and educational program, a number of considerations required careful planning. Because the system was intended to yield data regarding both student achievement and the quality of educational programs, it required a design that protected against a common confoundment. A problem with many accountability systems based on standardized student achievement test scores is that the tests are not constructed such that aggregated scores for individual *students* support valid inferences of *program* quality. Requiring schools to look good on the basis of individual scores frequently results in inflated results or "score pollution."[2] Test scores can be raised in a variety of ways *without* a rise in achievement. For example, curriculum and pedagogy can be aligned with test content and format—"teaching to the test," a now-hackneyed charge—in effect, investing test developers with not only the authority to monitor achievement but to determine the content and methods of teaching. With large-scale testing, the alignment mechanism is increasingly standards, and efforts are made to align curriculum to standards and to align tests to standards—presuming that the standards are satisfactory, that the curriculum will be appropriate, and that the tests and curriculum will be satisfactorily aligned. Curriculum developers and test developers should, of course, work together, but there is evidence, in these days of test-driven accountability, that assessment specialists dominate the work[3] and that curriculum suffers.[4] At Emily Dickinson, an assessment system was needed that did not distort the carefully crafted educational system in the process of assessing individual students and simultaneously providing evidence of the quality of its educational program. This was a major issue from a measurement standpoint.

For school personnel, other issues were more critical. They wanted an assessment system that was simultaneously coherent, consistent, and comprehensible for parents with children in more than one classroom, as well as for the children and teachers, and flexible enough to accommodate comfortably the school's variety in grade levels, subjects, teaching styles, and—important in a highly inclusive school—diverse students. They wanted the entire school, not just a pilot unit, to implement the new system together, which meant working with both the enthusiastic members of the school's vigorous assessment committee and reluctant teachers. They wanted parents to approve—which meant, in part, that the system needed to provide strong measures to protect the privacy of student work and to exhibit face validity—and they wanted to invite parents to take a sizable role in assessment, realizing that not all would do so. And of course, they wanted assessment that would fit with—not redirect or mangle—their curriculum and pedagogy and school goals.

The school's assessment committee studied R.O.P.E. and the portfolios of Vermont and Arts PROPEL in Pittsburgh,[5] developing an appreciation of a multitechnique assessment system and interest in portfolios, projects, performance tasks, and demonstrations of mastery. They wanted to use these techniques at all grade levels and in all subjects but recognized this was too much to try all at once (see Figure 6.1 and the assessment system design in Exhibit 6.1).

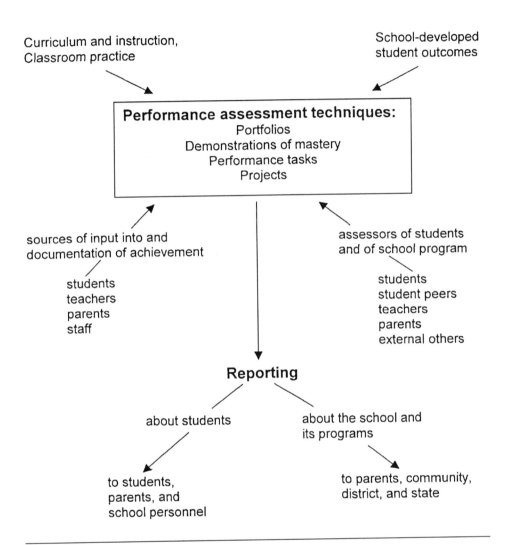

**Emily Dickinson Elementary School
Performance Assessment Program**
a three-year development

Curriculum and instruction,
Classroom practice

School-developed
student outcomes

Performance assessment techniques:
Portfolios
Demonstrations of mastery
Performance tasks
Projects

sources of input into and
documentation of achievement

students
teachers
parents
staff

assessors of students
and of school program

students
student peers
teachers
parents
external others

Reporting

about students

about the school and
its programs

to students,
parents, and
school personnel

to parents, community,
district, and state

Figure 6.1. Emily Dickinson Elementary School Performance Assessment Program:
A Three-Year Development Plan

Checking frequently with the faculty they represented, the assessment committee members agreed to an overall framework for gradual assessment development, building time into the design process to give themselves the opportunity to capitalize on emergent experiences and understandings rather than tying themselves down to a detailed plan developed when they were least knowledgeable and experienced about assessment. The plan provided that literacy portfolios would be introduced schoolwide in the first phase to be implemented in 1994-1995.

Our purposes for creating student portfolios

1. To document student achievement

    showing student process with one first-draft-to-final-product entry

    showing a range of accomplishment by including several products

2. To report student achievement to students, parents, the school, next year's teacher

3. To provide a basis for accountability

    for evaluation of the quality of EDES instruction, curriculum, school

    for the school (internal use), community, and district

4. To improve and individualize student learning

5. Other:

    To increase faculty dialogue

    To improve school unity

    To improve student self-esteem

    To provide a model for the district

    To improve community understanding of EDES

    To share ownership of student learning with the community

Contents of student portfolios

Guiding principle:

The portfolio should give as broad and accurate a portrait as possible of the student's strengths and weaknesses, progress over time, interests, range of accomplishment, individual and group effort, and ideas for future study. For these reasons, it should include work from early in the year and work from later in the year, successful work and work showing need for improvement to assist instructional planning. There should be opportunity for input by student, teacher, parents, and possibly others (e.g., teachers, specialists, student peers).

Portfolios should include:

5-15 entries at year's end

1 writing project in full (all pre-writes, drafts, edits, revisions, final copy)

list of student readings

"free picks": 2 by student, 1 by teacher, 1 by parents

reflections and self-evaluations by the student

evaluative comments and suggestions by teacher and possibly parents and others

---

Exhibit 6.1. 1993-1994 Portfolio Plan, Emily Dickinson Elementary School (EDES)   *(continued)*

Optional/ideas:

> narratives and anecdotal records by teacher, parents, and possibly others
>
> checklists of skills or assignments
>
> photographs
>
> audiotapes, videotapes (or references to class audiotapes, videotapes)

Method of selection of portfolio contents:

> The student and teacher jointly select entries for the portfolio, making the portfolio a "negotiated portrait" of student achievement. If the teacher and student disagree about whether to include a potential entry in a portfolio, the teacher takes final responsibility for the selection (exception: student and parent "free picks").

The EDES portfolio process

1. A student's work is collected in an individual folder.
2. Most work in the folder should have attached reflective-evaluative comments written by student and by teacher (optional: parent and peer comments).
3. At least 2-3 times per year, student and teacher have "review conferences" to review the work in the folder, to monitor student progress, to consider future directions, and to select work from the folder to go into the portfolio. Both adding and pruning of portfolio contents may occur at these review conferences.
4. At the end of the year, student and teacher hold a last review conference to determine final contents plus "free picks." The teacher tags two entries to be archived. These entries indicate such things as student progress over time, classroom activities, vivid examples of student accomplishment. In addition to student work, entries might include anecdotes, narratives, reflections, other commentaries; written, visual or audio records.
5. At the beginning of the next year, the next teacher reviews the portfolio to become acquainted with student achievement, interests, and learning style. This teacher duplicates the two tagged entries (including any reflective-evaluative comments that may be attached) and archives them for purposes of school accountability. This teacher returns the portfolio to the student, the ultimate owner, to do as he or she wishes.

Privacy protocol—providing access to portfolios while protecting the student's right to privacy

> Students and parents will be notified in writing of the portfolio access policy described here, signing their agreement and consent to participate.

Exhibit 6.1. Continued

Free access to a student's portfolio to
  student-owner
  student's teacher
  principal
  parents to their child's portfolio only

Controlled access via student permission to a student's portfolio to
  other students

Controlled access via teacher permission (or via principal permission if teacher is unavailable) to a student's portfolio to
  other teachers
  specialists, counselors, paraprofessionals
  visitors to school

Controlled access via principal permission to
  district personnel
  state personnel

Public exhibition of portfolio requires advance written consent of student and parent.

Notes

This plan provides for documenting student achievement. Methods of assessing portfolios will be considered in 1995.

This plan is for literacy portfolios (writing, reading, speaking, listening). Other subjects will be considered for portfolio documentation and assessment in 1995.

This plan is intended to provide a framework of broad guidelines, leaving opportunity for each teacher to adapt to students and styles, to organize contents, to determine formats for reflective-evaluative comments, and so on. The EDES assessment committee considers the planned portfolio program moderately structured.

Exhibit 6.1. Continued

The Literacy Portfolios and Process

Vermont's standardized writing portfolios were taken as a caution, almost a reverse guide. Like Vermont, Emily Dickinson wanted to encourage and strengthen student writing. But where, in Vermont, the state had specified what must be in a writing portfolio, Emily Dickinson wanted to avoid rigidity about contents. Where Vermont portfolios were essentially best-works collections, Emily Dickinson wanted a range of student work to enhance understanding of a student's strengths and weaknesses for curriculum planning. As they had seen in the Pittsburgh process-folios, they wanted documentation of one work-in-full to include every step in the writing process from the first idea recorded on paper, through every draft, to the final product, revealing the student's writing process, response to critique, and editing skills. For their literacy portfolios, they wanted more than writing—they also wanted evidence of reading, speaking, and listening.

In assessing the portfolios, where Vermont had required attention to a rubric with five rather simplistic criteria to be measured on a 4-point measurement scale, Emily Dickinson admired the feedback of the Pittsburgh system in which evaluation and feedback were narrative in character, more holistic and more detailed than anchored scores, more attentive to the actual features of student's writing than to prespecified criteria, and more likely to involve different criteria for different students and more than five aspects. Where Vermont required teacher-raters to agree or be retrained and had designed their portfolio system for high reliability, Emily Dickinson wanted to accept diverse opinions about the quality of student work from a variety of assessors, who would naturally operate from different perspectives. Where, except for a letter about the best piece, Vermont students were shut out of scoring, Emily Dickinson actively wanted student self-evaluation and peer evaluation.

The literacy portfolios would be shared with students, parents, the school board, and the community, in effect, offering the school's many audiences opportunity to assess student achievement as well. The basis for judgments of school quality would be archives of portfolio entries, which would reveal both the levels of student performance and achievement and the emphases and success of the school's educational effort. In addition to the archives, which could be accessed for scrutiny by state and district officials and others, reporting to external audiences (with safeguards to protect students' rights to privacy) would occur during parent conferences, where detailed examination of student records would provide parents with elaborated understandings of their children's achievements and of teaching emphases and effectiveness, and during more public occasions such as open houses or portfolio festivals. Emily Dickinson's plan for accountability echoed Pittsburgh's and anticipated House's[6] reconsideration of school accountability based on openness to public inspection rather than comparison of schools' test scores.

Although the purposes and needs and contexts were complex, Emily Dickinson's planned process for developing a literacy portfolio was simple. Student work and other achievement-related materials would be stored in a folder. To develop a basis for assessing oral presentations and other student work that would not generate paper evidence, the work of special students unable to express their achievement in writing, and collaborative student learning efforts, the materials in the folder might include audio- and videotapes and narratives written by adults familiar with student progress.

From the folder, the teacher and student together would decide which materials should be moved into the portfolio. This part of the process was envisioned as an exercise in teacher restraint of authority to ensure real participation by students. It was recognized that the desired student empowerment, encouraged by self-assessment, could be destabilized by teacher domination of portfolio conferences and student portrayals, effectively denying students ownership of their portfolios.[7] To ensure that a teacher could include an entry that he or she felt important, perhaps to identify student weaknesses, but to which the student might object, the teacher was granted a "free pick," which did not require the student's agreement. Parents were also allowed a free pick to ensure their opportunity to make the portfolio a well-rounded portrayal of their children's accomplishments and interests, which might well include out-of-school activities. Students were each granted two free picks.

Each piece in the portfolio would have attached reflective and evaluative commentaries—perhaps one, perhaps several; perhaps brief, perhaps detailed—from any of a variety of assessors. Students would be expected to self-assess, helping them develop understanding and articulation of their own work and progress, personal standards of quality, and responsibility for their educational attainment. Observing a privacy protocol (see Exhibit 6.1), students would also be expected to assess the work of their classmates, deepening their understanding of the possibilities for new directions and qualities in their own work as well as their appreciation of the capabilities of other persons their age, and refining their standards by applying and justifying them in assessing the work of others. Their teachers, other teachers in the school, staff (especially those offering special services to inclusion students), the principal, parents, and members of the school board and community might also offer commentary—again, observing a privacy protocol controlling access to the portfolio.

At the end of the year, the teacher would tag two entries in the portfolio for the school archives and give the portfolio to the child's next teacher. The next teacher would review the portfolio, gaining detailed understanding of the student useful for curriculum planning, then copy the two tagged entries, place the copies in the archives, and return the portfolio to its ultimate owner, the student.

At two pressure points in the process, flexibility was protected within an overall framework. First, Emily Dickinson teachers agreed all portfolios should include a reading list, a work-in-full, and the free picks, but beyond those six items, they wanted freedom to tailor contents to students and curricula. And worried that portfolios might grow so large as to make student conferences and pre-school year reviews unmanageable, they wanted a size established. So a range was set: a total of 9-15 entries, including the 6 agreed items and from 3 to 9 optional other items. Second, teachers disagreed about how often they should confer with each of their students to consider which entries in the folder might be moved to the portfolio. Grade level, subject area, and instructional and management practices suggested differences that the assessment system needed to respect. It was decided that a minimum number of conferences be established, two to three per year, a number which any teacher could exceed— and most planned to do so (see Exhibit 6.1).

Foundations

An underlying assumption of this system for assessing individual achievement is that diverse standards of quality are

Authentic	because standards vary in the real world outside of school
Natural	because each person individually constructs his or her standards, a constructivist perspective
Beneficial	because the offering of multiple assessment standards would generate closer examination of student work and deeper understanding of student achievement

No plan was developed for awarding grades or scores that would reduce feedback and foreclose on the consideration and discussion of each student's achievement. Rather, the plan was to examine the school's emerging portfolio culture at the end of the first year and to determine then how to translate the portfolio evidence of student achievement onto the school's unique report card.

Another assumption was that each student is unique and that *to reduce an evaluative judgment of his or her achievement to comparison to a standard,* as in standards-based assessment, *or to comparison to other students,* as in normative assessment, *was to deny his or her individuality and to overlook the singularity of his or her personal achievement.* The Emily Dickinson portfolios maximized responsive opportunities to portray actual student accomplishment, which located the system within the personalized assessment paradigm, and simultaneously maximized responsiveness to the curriculum, which also located the system within the contextual assessment paradigm.

Thus, the portfolio system design was attentive to four crucial purposes:

1. Documenting, assessing, and reporting individual achievement so as to support valid inferences of their achievement

2. Documenting and reporting the quality of the school's educational program

3. Providing an assessment system that supported and protected the school's ideology and practices

4. Providing a coherent structure with built-in flexibility to accommodate diversity among students and teachers

It was hoped the portfolio system, in practice, would serve as a non-obstructive organizer for the school's thinking and activities such that these purposes and the school community could be served.

Notes

1. During the 1992-1993 school year, as a faculty member at Washington State University–Vancouver, I consulted with the school regarding assessment development. The following year, Lake Washington School District hired an assessment specialist to assist all the district schools. The current Emily Dickinson system might well be quite different from the plan outlined in that first year, described here.

2. Haladyna, Nolen, and Haas (1991).

3. Très-Brevig (1993).

4. See Smith (1991).

5. Developed by the Pittsburgh school district with assistance from Harvard Project Zero and ETS and funded by the Rockefeller Foundation, the Arts PROPEL "process-folios" were embedded in an emerging portfolio culture in which students were reported to have developed professional-like thinking and work habits as well as strong motivation and strong relationships with teachers (Camp, 1990; LeMahieu, 1993; LeMahieu & Eresh, 1996; Rothman, 1992; Wolf, Bixby, Glenn, & Gardner, 1991).

6. House (1996).

7. The work of Leon and Pearl Paulson in Multnomah County, Oregon strongly advocated authoritative roles for students in producing their own portrayals (see Paulson & Paulson, 1991).

CHAPTER SEVEN

LEAP's Curriculum-Based Assessment of Integrated Curriculum Units

L EAP is the acronym for the Lake View Education and Arts Partnership, a group of four public schools in Chicago and the Chicago Teachers Center (CTC), two neighborhood arts organizations, and two community organizations first funded in 1993 by the Chicago Arts Partnerships in Education (CAPE) to promote integration of fine arts into academic subject matter. The partnership is an outgrowth of the earlier efforts of writer Jackie Murphy, who serves as LEAP program director, to motivate the development of writing skills by engaging students in playwriting. She and her partners saw theater as a vehicle for encouraging the students in their high-risk, multiethnic, multilingual urban neighborhood to develop important skills and to stay in school.

What has been called the LEAP "model" is simple: A teacher and an artist team-plan and team-teach integrated units. LEAP's multisession integrated curriculum lessons (ICLs) jointly focus on the academic goals of the teacher and the development of artistic and aesthetic skills in the artist's art form. Instructional teams are supported by a teacher liaison from each school, by coordination personnel from CTC, and by "weavers" to enhance continuity among units and connection to academic curricula and to encourage student reflection and writing. The arts content is intended to enhance the academic learning, and the academic content is intended to provide a focus for developing artistic skills, appreciation, and self-expression. The arts disciplines and the academic disciplines that have been combined for instruction in LEAP classrooms have included, among many others:

- Science and dance: On the topic of skeletal structure and physiology, students examined bones and studied the relationship to ligaments and other bodily elements in movement.

- Math and visual arts: Geometry students created optical illusions.

- History and textile arts: Bilingual students, many recent immigrants, studied the Bill of Rights and whether the rights promised were dispersed equally among people in the United States now and at the time of the authoring of the Constitution, then represented their understandings in a quilt.

- Theater and social studies: Small groups created countries with unique societies leading to understanding of the question, "Why is mass communication valuable?"

- Chemistry and visual arts: Students created mobiles to illustrate cell structure.

- English and visual arts: As part of a unit on Chaucer, students created illuminated manuscripts in tempera.

- Math and poetry: Lessons in algebra and rhythm were combined.[1]

When the program was evaluated at the end of its first year in 1994-1995,[2] evidence of educational benefit was already apparent. Since then, the success of the program has been recognized by different groups including, in 1998, Harvard's Arts Survive, which named LEAP as one of only eight "promising" arts education programs in the country.[3] Direct promotion of student achievement has occurred through lessons made more memorable by innovative format and personal connection to students' lives, an enhanced and expanded curriculum and pedagogy, and increased student expressiveness. Indirect promotion of student achievement has occurred through increased student participation and engagement, improved attendance, enhanced self-esteem and confidence, improved attitude toward school, and increased awareness of the local college where one of the LEAP partner organizations has maintained an office.

Teachers have also benefited in ways likely to improve educational opportunity. They have expanded their pedagogical repertoires and, to some extent, their views of their own curricula. They report feeling rewarded by students' improved learning. One, for instance, noted that his increased knowledge of students had led to formulating higher expectations of them,[4] a development often related to higher student achievement.

LEAP schools operate in a context of standardized multiple-choice testing. In Chicago, both state-mandated tests (Illinois Goals Assessment Program, IGAP) and city-mandated tests (Iowa Test of Basic Skills, ITBS) are required, and high stakes are imposed based on test scores. Despite the program's efforts and successes, one LEAP school has been placed on the city's infamous "watch list" because student scores have not been high enough, a move that threatens the entire faculty with firing. Teachers have been directed to aim their efforts toward direct instruction for the tests, which has sometimes involved forced rearrangement or reassignment of instructional time and abandonment of planned LEAP units.

In its third year, LEAP was expected by its funding agency to develop assessments for the ICLs. An immediate consideration was whether development of alternative assessments was a reasonable expenditure of personnel time, given the pressure of the standardized tests. Would evidence of student achievement revealed in teacher-developed assessments be credible in this locked-down testing environment? Deciding to do what they could to develop and implement curriculum-sensitive assessments while also trying to respond to the demands of the large-scale tests, LEAP arranged for professional development for teachers and artists,[5] which has included observation of LEAP lessons and the offering of suggestions teams might consider and adapt for assessing academic achievement, artistic achievement, and the other kinds of achievement they often hope to promote, such as teamwork skills and greater linguistic fluency with LEAP's many bilingual students.

The assessments have needed to reflect and evaluate achievement related to LEAP's specialized instructional units; that is, they need to be curriculum based. Operating primarily within the contextual paradigm, the assessments LEAP instructors have been encouraged to try, adapt, and develop often also provide opportunity to assess the individual understandings students gain in lessons, lessons that frequently call for the development of personal connection and personalized knowledge. So, as at Emily Dickinson, there is attention to two paradigms in the assessment system.

Unlike the single-technique literacy portfolios at Emily Dickinson, LEAP assessors have been interested in developing a variety of techniques including performance tasks, projects, demonstrations, discourse assessment, and direct observation of ongoing work. The nature of the content, skills, and instructional goals of the ICLs have largely determined which techniques are employed. Teams have been encouraged to try a variety of assessments, to develop multimethod assessment strategies to elicit valid inferences of the many kinds of learning expected of students participating in the units. Following is an observation of a LEAP unit and the assessment suggestions offered to the teacher-artist team. Other units and the assessments developed for them can be found on the LEAP Web site.[6]

Observation and Assessment Suggestions, November 27, 1996

Unit:	Creation and hero myths from different cultures
Subjects:	Anthropology and visual arts
Unit outcomes:	Illustrations of creation and hero myths
Grade:	High school, 17 students present, Lake View High School
Team:	Nancy Chapman, teacher, and Eduardo Angulo Salas, visual artist

Unit plans. The students have read creation and hero myths, written reflections in their journals, and developed their own hero myths beginning with a CTC-developed guided imagery activity. Nancy is developing a similar guide for creation myths. The class has discussed what is common among the myths. On the chalkboard are questions about the differences between commercials in the 1950s and today, about the universal elements of myths, and about their connection to Biblical themes. Nancy explained that personal application was desired, with students confronting the eternal verities: "Who am I? Why am I here? What, for me, is life? death? God?" Students were grouped for an earlier activity, each group to write a myth of each type, then to select one or amalgamate the two to write up and to illustrate. At the time of this observation, students were working on illustrations. An important unit connection: read, write, visualize; thus myth elements are to be evidenced in illustrations. Nancy had taken some photographs to document the process.

Special Considerations

Student considerations. Students were predominantly Hispanic. Nancy noted that the current class had worked well in groups, but a morning class had not. Nancy reported that her critique of student drafts had resulted in good one-on-one contact with students. Also, students had exhibited focus and engagement despite having a lot of work to do with such comments as, "This is my story!" "Did you read my story?" Eduardo confirmed that most students were enjoying the unit and understanding the main ideas, but reported that some lacked motivation due to "the unhappiness of their lives." He hoped that the unit would contribute to their self-discovery, development, and sense of personal power over their lives.

Teaching considerations. Nancy was interested in maximizing creative freedom and privacy and was willing to demonstrate flexibility and rule-bending to maximize creativity, which she felt was essential to maximize the benefits of the unit. Thus, the groups of the morning class had been disbanded in some cases, although Nancy had desired cooperative learning.

This unit was the most ambitious in terms of logistics and coordination of resources Nancy had tried. It involved arranging access and technical support for computer word-processing, movement of students between the classroom and the computer lab, availability of computer disks—as well as coordinating anthropology, writing process, and visual arts. In addition, the class was held in a "shared" classroom, requiring transport of unit materials and attention to cleanliness for the next teacher's class.

Nancy expressed interest in self-evaluation.

Classroom observation. Eduardo displayed the illustrations in Ezra Jack Keats's children's story, *Snowy Day,* and briefly discussed the illustrations. He later explained that he chose these illustrations because of their simple shapes and colors, which were amenable to collage and expressive possibilities and which were not intimidating to students who might feel reluctant about their artistic abilities. Even the collage covers of the myth writings were expected to have symbolic meaning. Students quietly began to work on illustrations using pencil, crayon, markers, magazine collage, and mixed media, with Eduardo circulating among them.

At the same time, Nancy met with students individually in writer's conferences, commenting on the substantive content of drafts, identifying difficulties related to clarity of explanations and character development and transitions, and offering suggestions. A few students left the room to work on computers to word-process the texts of their myths, which ultimately required finding a teacher on the second floor able to offer technical assistance and obtaining computer disks for students to store their texts.

Assessment Suggestions

Book reviews. The completed, bound, and illustrated manuscripts could be offered for review by a number of different assessors acting as "book reviewers." Assessors might include Nancy and Eduardo, other teachers, other LEAP partners, parents, and students including classmates. They might be asked to grade, to suggest grades for Nancy's and Eduardo's consideration, as well as to offer feedback to student author-illustrators. Reviewers might be undirected, as book reviewers commonly are, or they might be asked to consider particular points in their reviews, such as

Myth/text

Match to universal elements in creation and hero myths studied during unit

Theme/point

Plot plausibility or appropriateness to purpose

Character development

Fluency or vividity of writing style

Illustrations

Originality

Design

Craftsmanship or technical skills

Overall

Complementarity of text and illustrations

Construction of final product

Self-evaluation. If, at the end of this unit, students are to be asked to evaluate their achievement for the first time, it is likely that they will perform better with some direction. For example, a form could be prepared in which they are asked to respond to such questions as

---

Self-evaluation form for (name) _____

1. What did you learn about myths?
2. What do you think you will remember about myths? About your myth?
3. Did your study of myths help you see life (or your life) in a different way? Explain or give an example.
4. What did you learn about art?
5. Has this affected your thinking about art? or interest in art? or art activities? Explain or give an example.
6. What might have helped you benefit more from this unit? What more could have been provided? What more could you have done?
7. Is there anything else you would like to tell about what you got from this unit?
8. If you were grading your work in this unit, what grade would you award yourself? Why?

Peer interviews. Pairs of students could interview each other, given the task, "Find out how much your partner knows about myths." A first opportunity for peer assessment might begin with the class developing a list of questions (i.e., an interview protocol) to be used and adapted as students interview each other. Performance might be judged using a form such as

---

Myth Unit—Peer Assessment

Assessor _____   Assessee _____   Date _____

Questions (list of questions here)

    1.
    2.
    3.
    4.

Assessment (sample criteria)

Concept/ Topic	*Accurate and Detailed Information*	*Accurate Information*	*Too Short Information*	*Inaccurate Information*
Creation myths	_____	_____	_____	_____
Hero myths	_____	_____	_____	_____

Human characters	_____	_____	_____	_____
God/gods characters	_____	_____	_____	_____
Themes/ purposes of myths	_____	_____	_____	_____

Note: This activity would probably stimulate learning as well as assessment. Assessors would have to know enough to be able to judge the quality of their interviewees' answers. Assessors not well versed would probably have to request (learn) information from teachers or find it in other sources. Interviewees who believed assessors were failing to recognize correct answers would probably argue their answers were correct, leading to discussion and confirmation of correct answers.

Art assessment. Student achievement in art could be separately assessed by Eduardo and Nancy with comments to student-artists and possibly graded. The bound myths could also be offered for display with comment sheets on which audiences (perhaps classmates, if this were an in-class activity) could record their reactions or evaluations.

For other LEAP units, assessment suggestions have included

- Cartooning stories to assess young students' recognition of plot sequencing and reading comprehension
- Videotaping dance and drama performances, then using the videos as a basis for group discourse self-assessment
- Forming student assessment teams and (1) having students negotiate assessment criteria with instructors and then apply them in assessing classmates; (2) having students define assessment criteria and then apply them in assessing classmates; or (3) rather than criterial assessment, asking student assessment teams to make and then to justify evaluative decisions.

Teacher-artist teams have been encouraged to identify assessable activities and products within their units as compared to creating separate assessment activities. This enhances both the feasibility and the curriculum-sensitivity of the assessments.

Notes

1. Source: What is LEAP? What have we been doing? (program document).
2. I evaluated LEAP that year in one of several case studies of partnerships funded by CAPE. The evaluation was conducted under the auspices of the North

Central Regional Educational Laboratory (NCREL) (see Mabry, 1995b, 1997a, 1998).

3. Harvard Project Zero (1998, p. 2).

4. R. Schlichting, Blaine Elementary School teacher-liaison, personal communication, April 28, 1995.

5. I have worked with LEAP personnel for four years at this writing, from 1995, to develop unit assessments consistent with program and instructional goals.

6. LEAP's Web site: http://orion.niu.edu/~daflatle/leap/menu.html

CHAPTER
EIGHT

Walden III's Rite of Passage Experience (R.O.P.E.)

The full name of the school is Walden III Alternative High School: In the Process of Discovery. Located in Racine, Wisconsin, Walden was established in 1971 at the request of a group of teachers headed by Gerry Kongstvedt, Jackson Parker, and David Johnston. After meeting together for two years to try to meet the needs of students who seemed ill served in Racine's three large public high schools, they asked their school board for permission to start an alternative school. In the first year of the new school, the teachers realized their students needed a different kind of assessment, and they began to develop the Rite of Passage Experience (R.O.P.E.).[1] In the quarter century that followed, all Walden students—about 50 graduates per year—have been required to successfully complete R.O.P.E. in order to earn a high school diploma. This graduation requirement makes R.O.P.E. a high-stakes assessment for students.

R.O.P.E. works partly because it is an unusually student-centered assessment system in an unusually student-centered high school small enough to ensure strong familiarity among students, faculty, and staff. More than the curriculum, the philosophy and the practices of the school culminate and are reflected in R.O.P.E., a year-long assessment program for seniors. Resolutely committed to the multifaceted development of individual students, the school exhibits a number of features that encourage their individuality and initiative, applaud their political action even when it is inconvenient for school personnel, and require uncommon student responsibility for their own educational attainment and for their school's viability. Tolerance of student diversity and autonomy is high, as is the freedom and authority accorded to students. Demands are few but deep. All this is reflected in an assessment system that not only measures student achievement, not only promotes and provides education during the assessment process, but also finalizes the student's self-transformation from child to successful adult—a rite of passage in the anthropological sense.

Walden's student body has predominantly included two groups: (1) different-drummer students who don't easily fit into the high-compliance requirements of large high schools, kids who are independent, creative, outspoken; and (2) students with histories of academic failure and personal difficulties of all kinds, kids who haven't done well and some of whom would no longer be welcome at other schools. A few years ago, to maintain accessibility to the student population to which it has remained committed, Walden chose to remain in its high-crime, inner-city location even when offered a glamorous lakeside campus in a former religious institution donated to the Racine Unified School District.

Students come to Walden by choice, and they remain by choice provided they follow two rules: You can't fight, and you can't fail. Most students love, really love the school, but they and school personnel are quick to say it isn't a school for everyone—you have to take responsibility to make it at Walden. Not everyone stays, and some even leave after their junior year to avoid the rigors of R.O.P.E., the assessment system that inspired spin-offs by Ted Sizer's Coalition of Essential Schools[2] and Deborah Meier's Central Park East Secondary School in East Harlem, New York City.[3]

The Assessment System

In the Fall semester, Walden seniors take a R.O.P.E. class, which requires completion of the first two components of the assessment: a portfolio and a research project in U.S. history. When the assessment system was comprehensively studied in 1991, the portfolio included

- an autobiography;
- an employment history or résumé and letters of recommendation;
- a bibliography of all the books the student had read during high school except textbooks, a list of regularly read periodicals and newspapers, perhaps a list of books the student wanted to read, and two mini-book reports;
- an essay on ethics summarizing the student's personal code of ethics;
- an essay on fine arts including the student's standards of aesthetic judgment;
- an essay on mass media;
- an essay on human relations;
- a report of a science experiment conducted by the student;

- a science and technology essay; and

- an essay on computers.

Portfolio entries were graded individually by R.O.P.E. class teachers, and the overall portfolio was also assigned a grade. For students, writing the autobiography tended to be a profoundly affecting experience, for which teachers encouraged both creative options and deep personal reflection. All the entries promoted a kind of personal stock-taking, a multifaceted self-evaluation not only of students' academic skills but also of themselves as persons, oriented toward their preparedness for the adult world. In large part, the portfolios served as a springboard to get students thinking about their demonstrations of mastery.

During the Spring semester when there was no R.O.P.E. class, students were to demonstrate mastery in 16 areas:

English	mass media
reading	human relations
mathematics	U.S. history
government	science
self-expression	multicultural awareness
personal growth	world geography
ethics	personal proficiency
fine arts	physical challenge (PE)

Notice that these areas, some of which are virtually never formally assessed in other public schools, suggest the Walden belief that adult competence is more than a matter of academic knowledge and skill. In many of these areas, no class would have been offered, demonstrating the school's confidence that students would learn many important things on their own and also raising issues for explicit consideration and discussion as part of the life of the school. Students were required to attempt all 16 areas and to pass at least 12 to graduate.[4] With only the *R.O.P.E. Handbook*, a deliberately sketchy guide, students essentially confronted a momentous ill-defined task in each area: "What do I know about science (for example)? Do I know enough to be ready to pursue my personal goals after high school? How can I demonstrate to my R.O.P.E. committee that I know enough to graduate?"

R.O.P.E. committees included four members. The student's home-group teacher, whom the student might have known for as long as six years if the student entered Walden as a middle schooler, was an automatic member. Each teacher had a R.O.P.E. partner, so the home-group teacher's partner was also a member of a student's committee. The student chose the other two members: a junior and an adult from the community, perhaps an employer, minister, neighbor, parent, or Walden alumnus. No two committees ever had the same members, although any number of committees might have the same two teachers. The student had to schedule committee meetings, determining the timing and order of presentations and coordinating them with faculty availability and times the external adult, usually needing time off from work, could attend.

The teachers were, of course, familiar with R.O.P.E. but the external adults and the underclassmen, who were learning about R.O.P.E. expectations as well as assessing the seniors, were less familiar. No training was provided, and committees worked without scoring guidelines or rubrics of any kind. It was expected that they would make determinations of student competence on a case-by-case basis, drawing on not only what the student presented but also on their familiarity with the student's work and conduct in other times and settings. They were expected to explain and justify their decisions individually and, ordinarily, to reach a group decision, either awarding a grade or pass-fail according to committee preference. Teachers could remember rare occasions on which members had not agreed, and more than one grade had been recorded rather than averaging or forcing consensus. They also remembered a few occasions on which an additional assessor with expertise related to the student's demonstration had been invited to join a committee, but mainly they functioned as generalists who had gained enough from their own educations and professional experiences (including learning from R.O.P.E. and from each other) to judge competence at the high school level.

Intuitively, each committee developed personalized standards for each student, tacitly negotiating between ideas about what every high school graduate should know and about what the student they were assessing would need to know to succeed at his or her postsecondary goals and given his or her personal circumstances. They were observed setting higher academic standards[5] for a college-prep student than for a special education student, higher academic standards for a student planning to attend a major university than for one planning to be a horsewoman, responding to the level of competence students would actually need. These were high standards for all, rigorously applied to ensure students' preparedness and success when they left Walden's friendly confines. In about a third of the presentations I observed, students were not passed by their committees but, rather, were required to "re-do," sometimes more than once, putting pressure on committees as well as on students. But they were not identical standards for all.

Evidence of Assessment Quality

Evidence of validity was of many types and was very strong.[6] Validation is a matter of argument, not proof,[7] and some readers might consider the evidence of R.O.P.E.'s capacity to support valid inferences and actions inconclusive. However, some of the criterion measures against which R.O.P.E. results might be compared in an argument for the system's predictive validity are such cherished educational outcomes that the argument cannot easily be dismissed.

The construct at the heart of R.O.P.E. was achievement. The standard that a student had to meet to pass was a combination of a general concept of competent adult functioning and an individual concept of readiness for the student's own postsecondary goals. That graduates functioned competently in the adult world was abundantly evident in information like the following:

Statistics reported by the school district regarding employment of graduates from all local public high schools indicated that Walden alumni earned higher salaries than those from Racine's three large high schools.[8]

A recent graduate sent an articulate letter to the editor regarding community hiring policies for AIDS victims.[9]

The public testimony of parents regarding the level of their children's achievement included: "My daughter came here as a girl four years ago and is leaving as a young woman." And "I wanted my daughter to be an individual and to speak her mind. Robin has both." And "Walden taught Laura to be herself and gave her the opportunity to be independent. . . . Walden turns out adults, not 18-year-old children, and that's what it's all about."[10]

That graduates were prepared to succeed in pursuing their own goals, even as their goals evolved, was abundantly evident in both quantitative and qualitative data like the following:

Walden students earned higher composite ACT scores than did students in other Racine or Wisconsin public high schools.[11]

In 1984, the National Science Foundation awarded 540 doctoral scholarships in the areas of science and math, 13 in Wisconsin, and 2 in the most populous southeast Milwaukee-Racine-Kenosha area. Both went to Walden graduates.[12]

Between 1977 and 1986 at the University of Wisconsin at Madison, Walden graduates earned the highest average first-semester freshman grade point averages of alumni from all high schools sending at least five students to that institution.[13]

A U.S. Navy recruiter who had worked with local high school graduates for three years predicted success for his 1991 Walden recruit, who happened to be the student about whom teachers had expressed the most concern regarding possible R.O.P.E. failure. Walden students, he said, "seemed more aware than others [their] age that [they] had to get going on some type of career. I would say more mature." He attributed this maturity largely to R.O.P.E. "The R.O.P.E. program deals with actual life."[14]

A Walden graduate employed as a construction worker described his recent promotion: "There's seven business agents from Racine, Kenosha, and Walworth County, and they rate all these [applicants] once a year. I went in front of the union two times. The first time, I scored real low. After I walked out of there, I was like, 'Whew! Man, that was just like a R.O.P.E. meeting! Well, I'll get them next year.' So I brushed up and got all my stuff together, took more schooling down at Gateway [Technical College], just to show the union I wanted to improve myself. Last year, 40 people went in front of the union board. I just went in there and had all my stuff together, a folder full of papers. I laid it all out, all my hours from shop time, all my transcripts from Gateway. There were 19 people that made it. I took the first position."[15]

A mother who thought her son, a Walden graduate who attended the University of Chicago, had taken advantage of the school's flexibility to avoid difficult coursework he later needed, recognized that her son's ability to self-assess and his initiative, both promoted by R.O.P.E., had allowed him to self-remediate and succeed in an intensely academic university environment: "I think he was really prepared for college. He has that ability to be part of a discussion and to think and to express himself. I think a lot of that came out of [his] experiences. They weren't just, 'Give us the right answer' kinds of conversations at Walden. It was, 'Think it through. Present your point of view.' . . . When he looks around him, he seems to have been a lot better prepared than a lot of kids. He had to take a course and learn chemistry [which I think he should have done at Walden but didn't]. But thinking skills, being able to analyze something, to present his ideas in a clear manner—he knew *that* day one. He can learn chemistry."[16]

Does adapting standards to students' own goals inhibit them if they later decide on more ambitious academic plans? "I waited eight years before I went [to college] after I graduated. I kept saying I wished I had knuckled down and applied myself [in high school]. But I hadn't and, for a while, I was blaming Walden, that they didn't prepare me. I had never taken geometry. My mom and dad always tease me that I got a needlepoint degree at Walden, because I did learn needlepoint. [But] I think it all depends on the kid. You could take science. I could have taken anthropology. . . . On a scale of one to ten, preparation for life? Ten. I really would [give Walden that rating]. . . . Walden was like college. That's what, I think, prepared me the most." This report came from an alumna who completed college 15 years after graduating from Walden and who had not initially planned to go to college.[17]

Such evidence suggested that assessors' inferences and the act of graduating students that manifested those inferences were substantially valid. The record is the more impressive because of the characteristics of the student population. The 55 seniors in the class of 1991 included 24 who had transferred to Walden from other high schools, at least 9 with records of significant academic difficulty or failure, and 4 with retentions at the high school level and more at the elementary level.[18] Many were jeopardized by family disarray, drugs, and other serious difficulties. It appeared that about half of Walden seniors fit the label "at-risk."

Evidence of consequential validity was overwhelming. Especially considering the Walden student population, educational outcomes like those indicated above suggest that the contribution of R.O.P.E. to student achievement was enormously positive. Students routinely credited R.O.P.E. as significant in their development of needed responsibility and skills. A member of the class of 1991 wrote during her freshman year at college that R.O.P.E. had led to her

> being prepared for college not just with a lot of facts and figures, but with the ability and the academic maturity to go and learn more. . . . This semester I took a politics class, and was amazed at how many R.O.P.E. topics and terms were covered in the first few weeks. When some ideas were new and foreign to my classmates, I already had a grasp on the concepts, and for that I am thankful for R.O.P.E. That, and I'm about the only one who thinks nothing of having to write papers on a weekly basis! . . . It prepares the student of any caliber for "the real world"—both in college and society.[19]

The educative benefits of R.O.P.E. were readily apparent as students set new learning goals for themselves in preparation for demonstrations of mastery. Some who had failed classes took the initiative to learn previously missed material to pass R.O.P.E. Often, those who began self-remediation to pass R.O.P.E. ultimately changed their goals to learning what they needed to know for themselves. Said the oldest student in the class of 1991, a student whose academic record was so troublesome that she was no longer welcome at the high school she had attended before coming to Walden:

> I started [research for my demonstration of mastery in government] by looking through encyclopedias. When I found the information, it wasn't hard to understand, just splotchy, not really informative. So I went to the government teacher and borrowed books. I went through some of them. One was really good. It gave everything in detail. I read through the whole thing. It was interesting. It did take a lot of time, though. . . . [I]f they asked me questions about specific things like the bill of indictment and the plea bargain, I was ready to go into detail.[20]

The proportion of the adult citizenry of this country "ready to go into detail" about such matters is not impressive, suggesting a relatively high level of expectation of Walden seniors. Reports of the rigor of R.O.P.E. assessments were almost unanimous, indicated in such comments as the following from the same student:

> I have to tell you, R.O.P.E.'s an experience. I've heard some college students go through the same thing but without the personal stuff. R.O.P.E. is very difficult—all the research and preparation you have to do. Many things I prepare overly. A lot of time, staying up until three in the morning—it cuts out of your social activity. I could have done a really cruddy job [in R.O.P.E.] and not worried about how well it was done, but I wanted a good grade. I wanted a seal. I wanted to make a good effort. Grades were never important to me before.[21]

In terms of consequences to the school as a system, a founder summed up the general faculty feeling of the importance of R.O.P.E. to the school's philosophical coherence and practical focus by describing it as "the glue for the rest of the program."[22]

Despite compelling validity evidence, the following characteristics suggested R.O.P.E. would fare badly in an analysis of interrater reliability: differences in assessors' areas and levels of expertise, lack of formal articulation or consensus about criteria and standards, lack of rubric or scoring guide, lack of assessment training, shared assessment history of the teacher-partners but lack of shared prior assessment experience among the full team, and the unpredictability of what the student might present. Students offered quite different evidence of their competence, bringing videos or newspaper clippings or work samples, preparing charts or historical timelines or speeches, juggling during one demonstration of personal proficiency, formatting another presentation as a game show, critiquing artworks including their own, discussing science experiments, calculating on the spot the cost of recarpeting their bedrooms in response to a practical application often posed by committees, playing a jazz riff on the saxophone. Yet interrater reliability was extremely high in every observed assessment episode, not a single instance of score variance great enough to constitute unreliability according to the operational definition formulated for Vermont portfolios.

It appeared that validity was so strong it carried reliability with it. Note the implications for the theoretical relationship between validity and reliability. Whereas reliability has traditionally been considered necessary but not sufficient for validity, there was the strong likelihood that R.O.P.E. would exhibit validity without reliability. This possibility suggested that reliability might be neither necessary nor sufficient for validity, that validity and reliability were more independent concepts than previously defined. The influence of one of these psychometric properties on the other seemed to be the reverse of the accepted conception, strong validity having a positive effect on reliability (without being necessary for it)—the more detailed the evidence of competence, the more valid the inferences of achievement; the stronger the validity, the more obvious the student's level of competence and the more likely consensus among assessors regarding their judgments or inferences of competence.

R.O.P.E. had unusually strong validity and unusually strong reliability, stronger than many tests and testing programs. Moreover, R.O.P.E. revealed that the nature of the relationship between these concepts had been mischaracterized in traditional psychometrics. R.O.P.E. showed that hardworking teachers dedicated to their students as individuals could, through lived experience, intuitively develop a grasp of important measurement principles unavailable to theoreticians.

Feasibility

The longevity of R.O.P.E. indicated its viability, but the assessment system imposed strenuous demands on students and the school community. Teachers estimated, probably conservatively, that each senior required a minimum of ten hours of each committee members' time to complete demonstrations of mastery, not counting time for informal coaching and feedback. For a teacher, this amount of time had to be found for each senior in his or her home-group plus each senior in his or her R.O.P.E. partners' home-group, a total of perhaps eight in a semester. Teaching burdens were already unusually high at Walden, where teachers had fought their own union for the right to teach more classes than had been negotiated with the district—this so that Walden's small faculty could offer a large, appetizing array of courses in response to diverse student interests. For external adults, R.O.P.E. time usually had to be carved from work schedules.

The teachers said any teacher could "do R.O.P.E.," protested that they did not possess more than ordinary intelligence or skills. But they certainly were extraordinary in their commitment to students as individuals, to the maintenance and improvement of a strong and beneficial assessment program, and in the time and energy they wholeheartedly devoted to assessment. The affirming, motivating, confidence-building attention they lavished on students was promoted by a school population small enough to fit the descriptor, "the Walden family." Their familiarity with students enhanced the validity to be found in the assessment system as well as enhanced the general climate of honesty and trust, which also enhanced validity. A teacher said, "There's no better way to get to know a kid than to sit with them through ten hours of R.O.P.E. presentations. . . . Walden gives teachers a unique opportunity to get to know kids, and we appreciate that." Students said, "You can't get away with anything here. They all know you too well." Students were frequently overmodest in their claims of accomplishment, more often underestimating than exaggerating their competence. In the entire history of the school, only a single instance of cheating in R.O.P.E., a case of plagiarism quickly recognized, could be remembered.

That feasibility was not an important consideration for Walden people was clear from their investment in (rather than desire to overcome) struggle. The student struggle to learn and understand, the adult struggle to understand and assess—Walden founder and R.O.P.E. developer Gerry Kongstvedt articulated a fundamental idea regarding the intellectual effort crucial to both learning and assessing:

> The important thing was getting people to discover for themselves, to look in a different way at something they'd been looking at all along. . . . Feeling that you understand works against the process of becoming educated. The best thing about Walden is that it's a confusing place. It forces you to discover.[23]

Few documents have been generated at Walden regarding R.O.P.E., an assessment system falling wholly within the personalized assessment paradigm. The *R.O.P.E. Handbook* is distributed at the school, and there are a few forms, including a description of R.O.P.E. attached to transcripts (see Exhibit 8.1) and an evaluation form for presentations or demonstrations of mastery (see Exhibit 8.2).

Walden III Alternative Secondary School
1012 Center Street
Racine, Wisconsin 53403
(414) 631-7000

Walden III, established in 1971, is a public alternative secondary school within the Racine Unified School District which enrolls approximately 350 students in Grades 6-12. Students who wish to attend Walden III Middle or High School must apply for admittance. Students residing within the boundaries of the Racine Unified School District are eligible to apply and can be accepted at any grade level. The student body reflects the racial and economic distribution of the school district as a whole. The District is something of a microcosm with racial and economic distribution close to the national average. The District is comprised of rural, suburban, urban, and inner-city components.

The philosophy of Walden III stresses the internalization of learning a strong personal interaction between students and staff. The obligation for each student is to assume a substantial responsibility for the consequences of educational choices. Basic skills in reading, writing, mathematics, science, social studies, values, and aesthetics are strong, inherent aspects of the total curriculum. The curriculum also offers the opportunity for advanced studies in all major academic areas. In addition, on-site seminars, independent study, field study, and enrollment in university or technical school courses are all encouraged and may be reflected in a student's transcript.

Organization and Graduation Requirements

Walden III is organized into three levels; 6th, 7th, and 8th grade students are in the Middle School, which meets with a team of six teachers for one-half of each school day to work on basic skills. During the remainder of the school day, the Middle School student may select from a number of classes which may include those which high schools students are taking.

Students in Grades 9, 10, and 11 focus on gaining broad content exposure and meeting district graduation requirements.

Seniors focus on Walden III's unique Rite of Passage Experience (R.O.P.E.) which requires a student to present evidence of competence in each of 16 areas which are broadly representative of the liberally educated person. Evidence is presented to a committee of two Walden staff members, a Walden student and an outside adult. Each presentation is evaluated and feedback is given to the senior student. The 16 areas of the Rite of Passage Experience are indicated on each senior's transcript.

In requiring completion of the Rite of Passage program, Walden III has gone beyond the minimum competency requirement of the District. Walden graduates must meet the minimum district requirements in course work.

Exhibit 8.1. Walden Transcript Attachment Describing R.O.P.E.   *(continued)*

Evaluation and Credit System

The academic year is divided into four quarters, separated by an interim period of 2 days. The basic credit unit is called an "evaluation" and represents .25 Carnegie Unit of study and is awarded on a quarterly basis in each course passed.

An explanation of levels of achievement and transcript equivalents are shown below. Walden does not give weighted grades.

A (Ex) = Indicates high achievement in skill, knowledge and effort. Outstanding work in all aspects of the course.

B (Co) = Indicates competent achievement in skill, knowledge and effort.

C (Sa) = Indicates work meeting expected standards in skill, knowledge and effort.

D (Su) = Indicates the lowest passing evaluation and represents a level or work which does not meet overall quality expected of a Walden graduate. This evaluation may represent a lack of effort rather than academic potential.

F = Indicates no credit earned.

Exhibit 8.1. Continued

R.O.P.E. Presentation Evaluations
(Individual Committee Member Form)

		Student	Committee Member
R.O.P.E. Area	Date	Evaluation	Composite Evaluation
1. English*	___	___	___
2. Reading*	___	___	___
3. Mathematics*	___	___	___
4. Government*	___	___	___
5. Self-expression	___	___	___
6. Personal growth	___	___	___
7. Ethics	___	___	___
8. Fine arts	___	___	___
9. Mass media	___	___	___
10. Human relations	___	___	___
11. U.S. history	___	___	___
12. Science	___	___	___
13. Multicultural awareness	___	___	___
14. World geography	___	___	___
15. Personal proficiency	___	___	___
16. Physical challenge (check off)	___	___	___

Comments:

Exhibit 8.2. R.O.P.E. Evaluation Form for Demonstrations of Mastery

SOURCE: Reprinted with permission of Walden III High School.

* The school district awards a diploma seal for passing minimum competency examinations in each of the four subjects indicated. At Walden, seals are awarded for passing R.O.P.E. in these areas.

Notes

1. I studied R.O.P.E. during the 1990-1991 school year. This description of the school and the assessment program is based on that study (see Mabry, 1992a, 1992b, 1995c). Some changes to R.O.P.E. were being formulated at that time under the leadership of teachers Al Clausen, Louise Jennings, and Judy Doherty. I revisited Walden in 1999.

2. Sizer (1984).

3. See Bensman (1995).

4. The district offered a minimum-competency exam in English, reading, mathematics, and government and awarded diploma seals to those students who reached or exceeded a cut-score. Walden students were exempt from this exam because R.O.P.E. covered these areas and more (and Walden students could earn seals through R.O.P.E.) but were exempt from no other district academic requirements or tests.

5. Standards for competent functioning as a citizen or for personal responsibility were more uniform than academic standards.

6. A fuller discussion of the multidirectional validation effort and analysis of evidence is available in Mabry (1995c).

7. See Cole (1988), Cronbach (1988), and Messick (1989). See also Linn, Baker, and Dunbar (1991) and Moss (1992).

8. Racine Unified School District (1990a).

9. Anonymous Walden graduate (1992).

10. Anonymous Walden parents, public testimony (May 23, 1991).

11. Forte (1991).

12. C. Kent, personal communication, March 30, 1992.

13. "Suburban Students" (1981) and "Grades" (1986).

14. L. Verburgt, personal communication, July 8, 1991.

15. W. Herman, personal communication, May 20, 1991.

16. J. Hershberger, personal communication, May 15, 1991.

17. B. Olmstead, personal communication, May 22, 1991.

18. C. Kent, personal communication, March 30, 1992.

19. Anonymous Walden graduate, personal communication, December 2, 1991.

20. Anonymous Walden student, personal communication, May 10, 1991.

21. Anonymous Walden student, personal communication, May 10, 1991. A diploma seal indicated mastery in a subject.

22. Parker (1991).

23. G. Kongstvedt, personal communication, May 23, 1991.

NINE

Eagle's Wing Projects

Between 1993 and 1997, a specialized unit of Hudson's Bay High School in Vancouver, Washington offered self-selected students an alternate way of earning course credit toward graduation. Drawing on the name of the school mascot, the unit was called Eagle's Wing.

As Walden teachers had done two decades earlier, Wing teachers spent a year designing a program for students who might be better served in a nontraditional, individualized environment. During the planning year, these teachers developed a blueprint for learning and assessment and created instruments to document and facilitate the educative and evaluative processes. Within two hours of the arrival of the first students enrolled in the Wing, the teachers demonstrated remarkable flexibility by deciding they needed to make major changes to their carefully laid plans. This responsiveness to students was evident in many more ways when, at the end of the first year, teachers described assessment under the Eagle's Wing.[1]

Students in the Wing took some courses available on a block schedule and could choose to take others, but they primarily accumulated course credits through individualized projects. In a real sense, the projects were the curriculum. Just as the projects were individualized, assessment of the projects was individualized. Project documents functioned not only as negotiated agreements specifying student work but also as articulations of the curriculum and as assessment instruments.

Working on their projects, students frequently needed to be in authentic off-campus settings, and the Wing provided unstructured time for information gathering and research activities around town. The open-campus policy of the Wing and the appearance of students off-campus raised some suspicion in the community that Wing students were not working when they should have been or were truant when they were not.

Although many students reportedly found the autonomy and opportunity to engage in learning that interested them motivating, some students were not ready to assume so much initiative and responsibility. The teachers told one particularly striking story, which spoke volumes about the personal difficulties many students face these days and about the teachers' own compassion and patience. They told of a boy who simply did nothing for a long time that first year. No project. No work. When the teachers gently, occasionally encouraged, he did not respond. "Any ideas?" they'd ask. "Need any help?" Then, "You don't want to hang around here forever, do you? You do want to graduate, right?"

Finally, the boy said, "Look, all I ever wanted to do was run a heavy equipment rental yard."

"What a great project!" they responded. They coached him through the development of a plan to visit heavy equipment rental yards, talking to owners and managers about such matters as capital investment and inventory, to visit bankers to discuss financing and economics, and so forth. At the end of his project, the enlivened student earned credit in mathematics, economics, accounting, and language arts.

Of their handling of his case and some others, the teachers quietly observed, "Some kids need time to heal." The assessment system showed traces of this attentiveness to young people.

Instrumentation, Evaluation, and Individualization

A variety of forms outlined the process:

- A *Project Flowchart* illustrated the basic steps from brainstorming group and individual projects to final presentation before authentic audiences, evaluation, and the awarding of course credit (see Exhibit 9.1).

- An *Individual Learning Contract* helped students articulate the initiating questions and expected products along with identifying authentic audiences and special resources needed (see Exhibit 9.2).

- A *Project Timeline* encouraged students to break a large project down into steps and to estimate the time needed for each step (see Exhibit 9.3).

- A detailed *Portfolio Checklist* suggested an evidentiary array to illustrate project-related achievement.

- A *Portfolio Quality Evaluation* form elicited student-constructed criteria on which the portfolio would be evaluated and offered 6-point scales for rating achievement in relation to each identified criterion as well as for an overall portfolio evaluation. Only three

(text continues on page 148)

PROJECT FLOWCHART

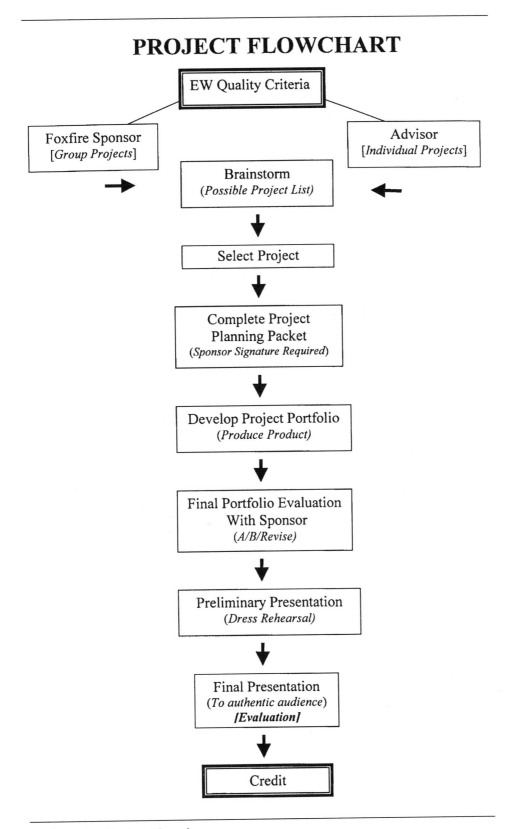

Exhibit 9.1. Eagle's Wing Project Flowchart

Project Title _____

Student Name _____   Sponsor _____

Step 2

_____ _____ _____
    Student ID Number   Beginning Date   Date Completed

○ 9
○ 10
○ 11
○ 12

_____ _____
_____ _____
Team Member Names

Individual Learning Contract

My question(s) is: (who, what, when, why, or how . . .)

The final product of this project(s) will be: (mark all that apply)

○ Report   ○ Video   ○ Photo Essay/Multimedia   ○ Drama
○ Interview   ○ Poster   ○ Model   ○ Recital
○ Demonstration   ○ Computer presentation   ○ Survey   ○ Other (describe below)

Does this project relate to a theme: □ Yes   □ No   **If yes, how?**

Who will be your authentic audience for this project?

Project Presentation: Date _____ **Location** _____ **Length of presentation** _____

Does this contract require the use of special resources, facilities, and equipment, or carry special legal implications?

□ **YES**   □ **NO** (If YES, attach permission form)

_____ _____
Student signature   Date   Sponsor signature   Date

Copy Distribution: White – **Advisor**, Gold - **Student**

Exhibit 9.2. Eagle's Wing Individual Learning Contract
SOURCE: Reprinted with permission of Vancouver School District.

Project Title _____

Student Name _____ Sponsor _____

Step 5

Project Timeline   Your plan for completing the project

Steps	**Est. Hours/Date Due**	**Approved**
Step 1		
Step 2		
Step 3		
Step 4		
Step 5		
Step 6		
Step 7		
Step 8		
Step 9		
Step 10		

Page ____ of _____ pages

Copy Distribution: White – **Advisor**, Gold - **Student**

Exhibit 9.3. Eagle's Wing Project Timeline

SOURCE: Reprinted with permission of Vancouver School District.

final grades were possible—A, B, or Revise—which suggested that high standards were expected (see Exhibit 9.4).

- An *Outcomes* form translated project achievement into course credit. For each project, the student identified courses whose content matched the opportunity to learn offered by the project, then noted what percentage of course credit he or she expected to earn at the completion of the project.

- A *Credit Justification Statement* at the end of the project documented the student's calculation of how much credit he or she thought justified by the work completed (see Exhibit 9.5).

- A *Progress Report* monitored progress toward course credits across the various projects in which a student might be simultaneously engaged, as well as progress toward project completion and the accumulation of credits toward graduation.

- A *Postproject Questionnaire* required students to evaluate their work, its contribution to their portfolios, and its contribution to their future endeavors (see Exhibit 9.6).

These forms reveal the high degree of individualization of learning and of assessment within the Wing. They also indicate significant sharing of authority for learning and assessment with students. The authenticity of activities and audiences and the opportunity for students to shape their secondary educations in the direction of their own postsecondary goals exhibited uncommon possibilities for enhancing student motivation and interest in education, especially perhaps for discouraged learners.

Differential Student Effects

As indicated earlier and as noted at Walden, student responses to the Wing as a program and the benefits the Wing extended to students varied according to individual differences. The Wing offered opportunity for personalized learning and personalized assessment, but students could fail to take full advantage of the possibilities. On the other hand, it is difficult for students who have personal encouragement from caring adults and who are surrounded by classmates excited about projects to persevere in resisting the chance to learn what they themselves think they need to know.

A high-achieving, college-bound sophomore related a different reaction. This student shared a large binder in which she kept information and a final report she had written as part of a project on a medical condition afflicting a relative. Her knowledge of this condition had become elaborated, as indicated by her discussion and her project documents, and had been beneficial not only to her understanding but also to that of her extended family. She had enjoyed being part of the Wing during its first year, she said, and felt she had greatly benefited in terms of knowledge,

(text continues on page 152)

Project Title _____   ┌─────────┐
                                                          │ Step   │
Student Name _____   Sponsor _____ │   7   │
                                                          └─────────┘

Portfolio Quality Evaluation

Other evaluator(s) _____
After each criteria title, evaluate 6 to 1 (6 being the best) and list supporting information.

Quality Criteria #1 -- _____	Supporting information:
	6 5 4 3 2 1

Quality Criteria #1 -- _____	Supporting information:
	6 5 4 3 2 1

Quality Criteria #1 -- _____	Supporting information:
	6 5 4 3 2 1

Quality Criteria #1 -- _____	Supporting information:
	6 5 4 3 2 1

Quality Criteria #1 -- _____	Supporting information:
	6 5 4 3 2 1

Quality Criteria #1 -- _____	Supporting information:
	6 5 4 3 2 1

Quality Criteria #1 -- _____	Supporting information:
	6 5 4 3 2 1

Quality Criteria #1 -- _____	Supporting information:
	6 5 4 3 2 1

Overall Evaluation   6   5   4   3   2   1

I should receive an overall grade for the activity of: ○ A   ○ B   ○ Revise

Copy Distribution: White – **Advisor**, Gold - **Student**

Exhibit 9.4. Eagle's Wing Portfolio Quality Evaluation Form

SOURCE: Reprinted with permission of Vancouver School District.

Project Title _____

Student Name _____   Sponsor _____

Credit Justification Statement

For each course title, list competencies that you have demonstrated in your project.
(*please use one of these sheets for each separate course.*)   page _____ of _____ pages

C O U R S E	

1. How much credit do you think your project work merits in this course?

.1	.2	.3	.4	.5	.6	.7	.8	.9	1.0

2. In your own words, explain why. (*review your outcomes page in the project packet*)

I have worked toward the attainment of the following **Learner Outcomes:**
(refer to learner outcomes section in the program guide, page 13)

a ☐   b ☐   c ☐   d ☐   e ☐   f ☐   g ☐   h ☐

Copy Distribution: White – **Advisor**, Gold - **Student**

Exhibit 9.5. Eagle's Wing Credit Justification Statement
SOURCE: Reprinted with permission of Vancouver School District.

Project Title _____

Student Name _____   Sponsor _____

| Step |
| 9 |

Post Project Questionnaire

Attach additional sheets
if necessary

1. How has this project added quality to your life?

2. Describe something about this project that you liked.

3. Describe something about this project that you didn't like.

4. What did you learn about yourself as you worked on this project?

5. How did you feel giving the project presentation? (*Be specific.*)

6. What did you think about the quality of your project portfolio? (*Identify its strengths, weaknesses, and how you would improve it.*)

7. How well did your team work together on this project? (*Describe the process of the project, the problem areas, and how they were resolved.*)

8. Will you continue with this topic in another project? If yes, what will you do next? If no, what are you interested in exploring next?

9. In what ways did this project fulfill the common characteristics that were identified in the Foxfire Instructional Model, step 2? (*page 18 in the program guide*)

10. List any community contacts you accessed to complete this project:

Site name _____   Site name _____
Contact person _____   Contact person _____
Address _____   Address _____
Phone # _____   Phone # _____

Copy Distribution: White – **Advisor**, Gold - **Student**

Exhibit 9.6. Eagle's Wing Postproject Questionnaire
SOURCE: Reprinted with permission of Vancouver School District.

research and project management skills, and development of initiative. Yet, with a heavy heart, she said she had decided to leave the Wing. "I'm just not sure that I'll learn everything I need to know from projects in order to make a good score on the SAT. I need a good score to get into college."[2]

This student's decision suggests a significant difficulty alternate assessment systems encounter. Even when these systems feature coherent practices well attuned to students, local contexts and opportunities, and theory, they nevertheless exist within a macroculture bound by assessment habits in contraposition to personalized assessment.

Notes

1. Three anonymous teachers, personal communication, May 1994.
2. Anonymous former student, May 1994.

Pan Terra's Learning Contracts

T he teacher-developed assessment system from which Eagle's Wing personnel had gained inspiration and ideas originated in small, nearby, alternative Pan Terra High School.[1] The school operated from various locations until provided a building in 1979. Named by its first students to signal a welcome to everyone "across the earth," the school's colors were the rainbow.

Most Pan Terra students were in need of a welcome. As at Walden, the school's program, organization, and assessment system were a carefully designed response to teachers' recognition of individual student needs. But whereas perhaps half of the Walden students experienced personal and academic difficulty, the vast majority of Pan Terra students were very much at risk. The approximate 40% drop-out rate at Pan Terra, published as part of the statistical profile of Vancouver Independent School District, did not encourage community confidence in the students or in the school. Not everyone understood that most Pan Terra students would have dropped out without the opportunity offered by the school to pull themselves together, that about 60% were essentially rescued, an extraordinary achievement. Few outside the school saw the efforts of students working through family disarray and abuse, supporting themselves with part- or full-time employment, shuttling between parents or extended family members, scrounging for housing and sometimes living in cars, battling addiction to drugs and cigarettes, dealing with pregnancies and babies and day care difficulties, coming back from the juvenile detention center—and trying to earn diplomas. Pan Terra housed the most bruised student body I had ever encountered.

The school responded to the complications in students' lives in several ways to facilitate their completion of high school.

Location. Besides the main program at the Pan Terra campus, there were branches at other Vancouver public high schools.

Scheduling and organization. The day program at the main campus offered some classes but mostly featured time on Mondays through Thursdays for teacher-student conferences, classroom space for individual study, computer lab facilities, counseling, and sponsored groups such as the Women's Group, most of whose members were pregnant or single mothers. In terms of staffing and class times, the day program (approximately 8:30 a.m.–2 p.m.) overlapped with the afternoon program (12:30–5:00 p.m.), which also overlapped with the evening program (6:00–9:00 p.m.), offering similar opportunities at a variety of times so that students could select school hours, perhaps to keep jobs as they earned credits.[2] In addition, the expanded campus program allowed students working full- or part-time to schedule appointments with faculty for contract development, consultation, and assessment.

Curriculum and assessment. Learning was focused by personalized education plans (PEPs) developed in conference with students, parents, and teachers (see Exhibit 10.1). Individualized learning contracts (see Exhibit 10.2), with some classes also, provided the means for implementing PEPs and for accumulating course credit toward graduation.

Assessment by Contract

Assessment of student achievement involved two steps. First, points were calculated for progress toward contract completion in a weekly evaluative conference with a day program student, the teacher taking primary responsibility for determining the number of points to be awarded. The amount of time the student had spent on contract-related work, the difficulty of the work, and the tangible evidence of progress were considered in determining point totals. The total number of points across all contracts that a student had earned during the week was forwarded to the principal for review. If students did not earn a minimum number of 250 points per week,[3] teachers added a note to advise the principal as to whether there were extenuating circumstances that suggested that a sub-minimum accumulation should be accepted for the time being or whether the student should be warned or, failing to improve over a period of time, dismissed. For example, on one occasion, picking up a note from his desk, principal Steve Friebel said,

> Here's a kid who hasn't been here for long. He and his teacher set a goal of 1,200 points per week, but he's making 1,000. The note says, "Needs a fatherly chat, Dad." Here's another who earned 812 points. The note from the teacher says, "She's OK for now." Here's

Student – Parent – Faculty
Negotiated Individualized Education Plan Form

Date of Meeting: _____   Time of Meeting: _____

Student: _____   For School Year: _____

S	C	H		GOALS	SUPPORTING INFORMATION
			Sciences		
			Humanities		
			Other (extended day)		
			Career Exploration Service Learning		
			Personal Development		

S = School
C = Community
H = Home
Participants' signatures:

To the satisfaction of the participants of the IEP team, projected start date for goals, person responsible for goals, and provision of related services have been discussed.

_____ _____

_____ _____ _____

Exhibit 10.1. Pan Terra Individualized Education Plan for Students

---

Pan Terra Alternative High School Learning Contract

Name (s): _____   _____
                                                                                                        Start Date

Teacher (s): _____   _____
                                                                                                         End Date

O
B
J
E
C
T
I
V
E

What:

Why:

Points and Credit Distribution

P
R
O
C
E
S
S

How:

How my teacher can help:

Conference Dates: _____   _____   _____

D
E
M
O
N
S
T
R
A
T
I
O
N

How I will show what I've learned:

How my teacher and I will know it is a quality accomplishment:

_____
                                        Student(s) Signature(s)

_____   _____
          Teacher Signature   Advisor Signature

Exhibit 10.2. Pan Terra Learning Contract

SOURCE: Reprinted with permission of Lewis and Clark High School (formerly Pan Terra High School).

another student with 868 points who had two weeks on jury duty, so he's actually done fairly well. Here's one I'll call in and ask, "What are you doing? What's the point of being here? Could you do this on a job?" It's to get her to make an effort, not to embarrass her; she's trying.[4]

Second, the point totals were translated into cross-curricular credits. For example, a student might work on an integrated contract that involved science, reading, and report writing, receiving points that would count toward credits in science and English. These credits accumulated so the student could ultimately meet district course requirements for graduation: 19 credits for older students whose classes had already graduated; 22.5 credits for all other students at Pan Terra and other public high schools in the district. Students were also required to pass a simulated version of the GED.

The intermediate step of awarding points offered a distinct benefit to Pan Terra students, most of whom had experienced extensive prior difficulty in school with consequent loss of confidence and self-esteem. The frequent point calculations gave students immediate feedback indicating successful progress, which aided motivation, and a regular means of figuring out how much work was left to be done, which encouraged goal setting and planning. There were no long periods in which an already discouraged learner might lose sight of his or her headway or might lose personal contact with an adviser. The awarding of points assured regular appraisal and interactive feedback in discussions described as "genuinely collaborative,"[5] and countered alienation or isolation through ongoing, individual connection to teachers and the principal.

The point system also made assessment somewhat mechanical and opened possibility for misrepresentation in two ways. First, it was possible for students to exaggerate the amount of time they had spent working on their contracts. This did not appear to be a strong threat to the validity of inferences of student achievement, however, because of checks built in to the system. For one, teachers expected to see tangible evidence of progress and, without it, were resistant to awarding credit. Also, as at Walden, the small size of the school engendered strong teacher-student familiarity and opportunity to note what students were doing. In contract discussions, exchanges like the following sometimes occurred.

Teacher Renée DeVore was calculating weekly points with Jeff, an eager, polite student. When Jeff reported time spent on his contract, some of it in Renée's classroom, she did not accept his estimate, gently but firmly recalling that he had been easily distracted. She suggested a couple of strategies that might help him stay on task in the future. Her colleague Anna Whipple came to report points for him on a contract with which she was helping. Looking sympathetic, Anna nevertheless reported fewer points than Jeff was expecting, explaining there had been some days Jeff's work had been hampered by his having a sore hand.

Jeff calculated the additional points in his head, "So, that's 226 points now." He sighed, looking crestfallen, then brightened, "You didn't take the points from my math," he reminded Renée.

"I'm waiting until it's finished," she said.

"It's finished!"

"Totally?" When he nodded, Renée responded, "Bring it in."[6]

Familiarity also contributed to trust and honesty, which had a transformative effect on students and a positive enhancement to validity in assessment. As one student described it,

In my early days here, I did some work, but I didn't get many points. I've seen it with other students, too, especially new students. Teachers know when you're trying to play a game, not doing your work. That's when they'll get on your case. The teachers will make it harder and harder for you to get away with stuff. They'll ask harder and harder questions. They'll take care of the situation.

You'll get a different kind of education here, a whole nother type of skill because we sat down and learned it—learned how to learn it. In a way, it's better, more independent, responsible, self-motivated—and that's a tough thing to be. I messed around before I got here; I have regrets. Without this school, who knows where I'd be? And I like where I am today. I may not be the most educated person, but I'm smart. And my smartness came from this school.[7]

These transformations, a uniform theme in descriptions from students and teachers, were not coincidental, and they contributed to accurate representations and inferences of student achievement. The principal explained the placing of educational responsibility with students as soon as they entered, in his description of orientation sessions:

They *can* cheat. And, if they continue to do it, they're out of here. We tell them, "It's your education. We have *our* diplomas. Our job is to get you ready for what comes next."[8]

The idea underlying this strategy was suggested by a teacher whose comment indicated not only faculty consensus on this point and Pan Terra's institutionalized compassion but also the mechanism by which students were empowered to transform their lives:

If a student wants to choose to not do a damn thing, he can do that, or she [can do that]. The point is there is a natural consequence for that, and the kid chooses to correct the consequences or not. It puts the responsibility for learning on the student. How can I be responsible for what happens in someone's head? That's an absurdity.[9]

The other possible distortion to assessment from the point system was that time on task was heavily credited in the awarding of points, enough that *time on task* might sometimes function as a rival construct to *achievement*. A recognized difficulty, the faculty and staff were working on this aspect (and other issues, such as responding to new state and district student learning outcome requirements called Essential Learnings) in a schoolwide, multiyear professional development program on the topic of assessment. At one well-attended, four-hour-long evening session, itself a testament to the faculty's dedication to good assessment, a teacher working on this issue said,

> The demonstration portion of the contract isn't adequate. It's tied to the fact that we give credit through points, which is kind of a phony way to do it—better than ABCs, but still—.[10]

In an interview three weeks later, another teacher acknowledged,

> To a lesser extent, awarding points does what grades do—puts the focus on completion instead of learning. We all agree that the point system is better than traditional grading, but we want it to be better. A few years ago, we looked at another way to chart progress, but we couldn't find one the public would accept—there's a lack of trust in teachers to accurately assess and evaluate. It's always subjective.[11]

The principal described this issue as perennial, resulting in annual redesign of the contract over a ten-year period and in increasing focus on the assessment portion of the contract.[12]

Like Walden teachers, Pan Terra teachers had developed and long practiced good assessment, and none of them seemed fully satisfied with it, consistent with a framed quotation from Thomas Edison in the principal's office:

> Restlessness is discontent—and discontent is the first necessity of progress. Show me a thoroughly satisfied man, and I will show you a failure.

At both schools, serious, long-term efforts were underway to improve assessments that were already admirable and far-sighted. In their evaluations of student achievement, like Walden assessors, Pan Terra teachers developed individualized standards for each student, balancing between what any citizen would need to know to function as a competent adult, what a particular student would need to know to be prepared for his or her postsecondary goals, and what achievement level was reasonable to expect given individual circumstances. The desirability and rarity of individualizing achievement standards were acknowledged by a teacher:

> Even the big high schools realize you can't treat all 28 kids in class the same—it's insane. They all know that, but they don't know how to do that [individualize standards] because [traditional assessment] is so institutionalized.[13]

But the differences in the student bodies of the two schools meant that data regarding Pan Terra graduates' postsecondary success might offer less impressive criterion-related evidence of the validity of assessment-based inferences. When asked whether a diploma from Pan Terra indicated or should indicate about the same level of achievement as a diploma from another Vancouver public high school, one teacher said,

> Our kids usually come with big deficiencies in many areas. For us to give the high school credits when they're doing work at third-, fourth-, fifth-grade level is a lie. This bothers me.[14]

On the other hand, students were required by the school district to pass a simulated GED exam. Another teacher stated,

> Some of the effort I see from students is not high school–level work, but sometimes that's not a realistic expectation. If a student is making a real effort but the work is not high quality, I'm going to encourage effort. It doesn't help to do otherwise. The first time, I'll give points if there is effort and improvement and I'm convinced they're doing the best they can do under the circumstances. I'll really scrutinize the time log and call them on it if they can do better. What else should we do? Have them work for two years and get no credits? It's not realistic to expect them to come to school and get no credit. But what does that say about the value of a high school diploma?[15]

In spite of this difficulty, student readiness to function in society was suggested by the jobs they held, by reports of the eloquence with which Pan Terra students had publicly argued for the reclamation of a natural environment near the school,[16] and by observations of the district's multigroup high school restructuring task force on which Pan Terra students repeatedly distinguished themselves from their counterparts from other public high schools by their articulateness.[17]

In contrast to the many documentary forms developed for Eagle's Wing assessments, Pan Terra's contract was a deceptively simple single page. Used in conjunction with the PEPs, the learning contracts were uncluttered with prespecifications, concentrating on fundamentals: the learning objective (what, why), process (how, how my teacher can help, conference dates), demonstration (how I will show what I've learned, how my teacher and I will know it is a quality accomplishment, points and credit distribution), start and end dates, and signatures. Admirable in its focus, conciseness, and flexible open-endedness, it looked like the perfect tool in the hands of Pan Terra's experienced faculty, but they were working to improve it, too, in their professional development program.

Feasibility

Where the time demands of R.O.P.E. on Walden's faculty were heavy because they came in addition to a typically structured school day and overfull teaching responsibilities, Pan Terra's school day was structured to prioritize contract-related work and consultation. As a result, one teacher reported that the demands on his time at Pan Terra were not greater than those he had experienced in traditional settings. Still, finding enough time could be a problem. Another teacher explained a solution also discovered by many of her colleagues:

> If I had had them all wait to develop written contracts, some students wouldn't have been able to get started on their projects at the time their ideas were exciting them. So we'll negotiate something verbal, which gets them moving. For a student I've worked with for a long time, the kid can just tell me an idea, and I'll say, "Go." I don't want to stop a student from getting started on an idea he or she is excited about.[18]

Feasibility was also enhanced by the relatively low paperwork burdens imposed by the school's assessment system and by the shared responsibility of teachers and students for documentation.

External Threat

The most serious threats were not to the validity of inferences and uses of assessments at Pan Terra but to their local credibility and vulnerability to top-down reform initiatives, like state and district Essential Learnings and mandated testing. Pressure from the district fluctuated, but approval was suggested by the school's new, well-equipped building, which opened in the 1998-1999 academic year.

Close up, Pan Terra students were engaging, human, admirable in their against-all-odds efforts; at the distance from which most of the community saw them, including the school board and school district personnel, Pan Terra students were the smokers at the edge of the schoolgrounds, the scruffy kids seen off-campus during school hours, the worst-looking statistics in the district. Amazingly, unfairly, but typically, institutions like

Pan Terra that shoulder society's most difficult responsibilities are often not recognized but suspect for their courage and efforts. Amazingly, unfairly, but typically, disadvantaged teenagers are often not recognized for their valiant struggles but suspect because of their obvious lack of advantages. If asked to describe the students or the school, most Vancouverites would more readily have raised doubt than proclaimed virtue. That Pan Terra would probably not have survived if the school hadn't improved district drop-out rates in its student reclamations was a probability not lost on the faculty, one of whom said,

> Someone needs to realize we're doing the best we can. These kids are becoming positive members of society. If we weren't here, the district and society would be losing them. This student population demands so much time.[19]

Systems That Fulfill the Promise

There are others,[20] but why aren't there more examples like these of assessment systems that are truly educational, that provide strong evidence of student achievement, that encourage as well as measure student achievement, and that support teachers as professionals rather than technicians? Why have some of these schools and their jewel-like programs and assessments met such intractable difficulty? How much could we accomplish if we offered all students such motivating, educative, self-enhancing assessment? What would high-performing students do with an opportunity like that provided Pan Terra students?

Perhaps the rarity and opposition are a sign of our intolerance for variance, our modernist obstinacy on finding and systematizing a right way of doing things, our insatiable craving for a simple answer, a bottom line. Bill Wiley, who had developed a school in Everett, Washington with a similar philosophy, a school at which some Pan Terra teachers had previously worked, said during a professional development session on assessment he offered,

> What you do in the classroom should not be dictated by somebody else's needs but by the needs of the students in the classroom. We need to find a way to keep people off your back and keep that process alive.[21]

These five systems counter the assessment habits of a century. They fall without a dominant paradigm that fails to recognize them. In the national mania for big schools and systems and consequent standardization, they dissent. These systems foreground formatively delicate young people and background constructs and content, rather than the reverse. They do not succumb to—and they protect students from—relentless insistence on comparison and competition.

In the United States, we have increasingly forced school reform through achievement testing, pressed toward lock-step educational surveillance systems, and instituted harsh sanctions.[22] Why do we tolerate policies and practices with inhumane and countereducational results? Why do we fail to notice the destructiveness of this Gordian knot? Unsatisfied, we have been more inclined to tighten up than to look elsewhere. We're not content with the state of education, with our test score rankings against Japan and Singapore,[23] with the preparedness of our workforce, or with progress toward our national education goals.[24] We're not nearly as pleased with assessment and educational outcomes as are Racine's self-proclaimed "walnuts" or Pan Terra's students and faculty, one of whom said,

> Teachers say they never see the rewards of their work. They look at their job as teaching the discipline or the curriculum. That's a mistake. The job is not conveying information. The job is helping them find information they need to fulfill their goals. Academic progress is incidental to the development of the entire human being—it's third or fourth on the list of things that matter. A girl leaving her boyfriend because he's beating her up is more important than making As and Bs—it's real growth. Or seeing some total screw-up kid who was headed for [prison in] Walla Walla instead walking down the mall with a wife and a kid and a haircut and a good job, buying a house, saying, "I'm here 'cuz my wife says I have to"—he's grown up and figured it out.
>
> It's very rewarding. Nothing works like a human relationship. It makes all the difference. It's the sine qua non of the job.[25]

People at these places and others have long-established track records of competent alternative assessment, deep and different understandings of assessment quality. They would not say everyone should do what they do, but what they do and what they know deserves attention and can enrich all our understandings and practices.

Notes

1. I collected data in May-June of 1997, in the last year before the name of the school was changed, first to Vancouver Personalized Learning Center, then to Lewis and Clark High School. The description here reflects the assessment practice of that time (see also http://www.vannet.wa.us/~panweb/).

2. The school permitted students to choose to stay on campus for longer periods (S. Friebel, personal communication, August 7, 1998).

3. Point logs, 10 points per hour, provided documentation that students were meeting the state of Washington's requirement for evidence of a minimum of 25 hours per week of student work.

4. Personal communication, May 29, 1997.

5. S. Friebel, personal communication, August 7, 1998.

6. Observation at Pan Terra, May 15, 1997.

7. Anonymous Pan Terra student, personal communication, May 13, 1997.

8. Personal communication, June 2, 1997.

9. D. Haggerty, personal communication, June 3, 1997.

10. S. Sevenich, comment during professional development session, June 15, 1998.

11. M. Barr, personal communication, May 29, 1997.

12. S. Friebel, personal communication, August 7, 1998.

13. D. Haggerty, personal communication, June 3, 1997.

14. D. Williams, personal communication, June 2, 1997.

15. M. Barr, personal communication, May 29, 1997.

16. L. Davies, personal communication, May 20, 1997.

17. Source: my observations in 1992-1994 as a member of the task force.

18. L. Russell, comment during professional development session, June 15, 1997.

19. D. Williams, personal communication, June 2, 1997.

20. Two well-known other examples in public schools are the K-8 assessments in the Winnetka school district in the Chicago area and the high school assessments at Central Park East Secondary School in Manhattan. At the college level, alternative assessments are long-lived at Evergreen State College, Antioch College, and Alverno College.

21. W. Wiley, presentation to Pan Terra Faculty, June 15, 1997.

22. See, for example, Indiana Education Policy Center (1994).

23. Among the many reports of substandard performance in comparison with other countries, see Manzo (1997).

24. The U.S. Department of Education, at the time of this writing, was receiving responses to a request for proposals (RFP) to measure progress on the national education goals.

25. D. Haggerty, personal communication, June 3, 1997.

THREE

The Portfolio Planner

As the examples in Part 2 suggest, a key to the success of alternative assessment systems is thoughtful consideration of particular purposes, contexts, styles, and students. In Part 3, the Portfolio Planner (see pp. 168-176) offers a step-by-step means of developing a portfolio system sensitive to such issues. With a bit of extrapolation, the planner can also guide the design of alternative assessment generally or can guide the analysis or reconsideration of an existing assessment system.

An important source in identifying decision points in the Portfolio Planner was the variety found in British and Australian profiles. Alternative assessment, as a contemporary phenomenon in the United States, is relatively new, with interest building from about 1990.[1] Because many efforts began about the same time, early developers have had few sources of information more knowledgeable than themselves or examples with more longevity than their own. As a result, looking to each other or to texts not much more familiar with the new ideas, many early systems exhibited both the constraints of an old paradigm and considerable similarity.

In Britain, the development of profiles exhibited more variety. In the mid-1970s to mid-1980s, a number of independent initiatives attempted to provide "school-leavers" who would not take the British version of college entrance examinations with some written record attesting to their achievements, alternatives to the test scores they would not have. These efforts resulted in the development of profiles, positively stated documents that detailed students' efforts and achievements and that might help them make a successful transition from school to work.[2] The business community supported these efforts.[3]

In 1984, the Department of Education and Science published *Records of Achievement: A Statement of Policy,* which encouraged local development of profiles or records of achievement (ROAs) and which stated the government's intent to required them for all secondary school students by 1990. The following purposes or features of ROAs were listed:

- to recognize and document students' achievements and experiences;

- to contribute to their personal development through increased motivation and awareness of strengths, weaknesses, and opportunities; and

- to inform curriculum, teaching, and organization so as to help students develop not only academically but also practically and socially.[4]

The government specified nothing about how ROAs should look or work. With the creative door open, schools and local education authorities (LEAs) responded with an enormous diversity of adaptations.

Profiles and portfolios share a similar aim, to offer an expansive view of student achievement, but they differ in the types of documentation they provide in their portrayals. Profiles are collections of statements about students, free-form narratives and forms specifying certain types of information, as well as records such as certificates. Contrastingly, portfolios are collections of student work that may or may not include statements by others or additional records.

But the wording, *collections of student work,* is deceptively simple. Which work? Best work, or work showing progress over time, or a range showing both strengths and weaknesses? Academic work only or other achievements, too? Only work that generates evidence on paper? What about speech, music, art, drama, group work? To document what the student has done or to assess it? Who should assess it—and when and how? Who gets to see it? Who should own it—does the portfolio belong to the student or the school? These decisions will all be made, either consciously or by default. The purpose of the Portfolio Planner is to support thoughtful design and practice.

One idea embedded in the planning strategy is that of planned emergence. In most cases, not everything in the eventual system should be attempted in the first effort. As with any new practice, change usually takes time, and it is easy to feel overwhelmed if too much is undertaken too soon. For most, it is likely to be better to concentrate on a few basic ideas initially, to learn through experience, to build the system gradually, to cultivate flexibility and expectation of revision and improvement along the way.

The Portfolio Planner can be used either by individuals or by groups of assessment designers, can assist with developing an assessment system for a classroom or for a school or for a larger educational entity. Discussion and feedback from colleagues is likely to encourage both good practice and feasibility for any assessment system, whether large or small in scope. Discussion with students is also likely to be helpful, generative of ideas and of useful considerations. Parents and others in the school community may also be productive sources of ideas and critique.

Thinking, discussion, keeping open the conversation about how best to assess, keeping open the conversation about what each child knows—educational assessment is well served by thoughtful deliberation, and students are well served by sensitive educational assessment.

Notes

1. Direct writing assessment, the most popular means of performance assessment in state programs, dates from before this time, however (Mabry & Daytner, 1997).

2. Broadfoot (1986, 1996) and Broadfoot, James, McMeeking, Nuttall, and Stierer (1988).

3. Law (1984).

4. Broadfoot (1986).

Portfolios in My Classroom: A Planner

1. Purpose. **What do I want portfolios to do in/for my classroom?**

I want to use portfolios	This Year	Next Year	Future
to document			
student achievement, effort, and progress	____	____	____
process as well as product	____	____	____
the development of one product in depth	____	____	____
to preserve successful, representative, or favorite work	____	____	____
to assess student achievement, effort, and progress	____	____	____
to help students learn to assess their own achievement	____	____	____
to report student achievement, effort, and progress			
to student	____	____	____
to parents	____	____	____
to the school	____	____	____
to the student's next teacher	____	____	____
to the student's prospective college or employer	____	____	____
to assist with student placement or course selection	____	____	____
to document or encourage diversity in student learning	____	____	____
to individualize student learning	____	____	____
to improve student learning	____	____	____
to evaluate			
quality of instruction	____	____	____
quality of program or curriculum	____	____	____
quality of education at our school	____	____	____
to provide information for school accountability			
internally, for school purposes	____	____	____
to the community	____	____	____
to the district	____	____	____
to the state	____	____	____
to accrediting agencies	____	____	____
Other uses or goals:			
a.	____	____	____
b.	____	____	____
c.	____	____	____
d.	____	____	____

2. <u>Contents.</u> **What will go into portfolios? Who will create and select the contents?**

	To be selected or created by	Student create	select	Teacher create	select	Other create	select
____	Students' best work (tests, papers, reports)	____	____	____	____	____	____
____	Unsuccessful products	____	____	____	____	____	____
____	Drafts as well as completed products	____	____	____	____	____	____
____	Required entries	____	____	____	____	____	____
____	Optional or nonrequired entries	____	____	____	____	____	____
____	Evidence of a range or accomplishment	____	____	____	____	____	____
____	Evidence of group work	____	____	____	____	____	____
____	Evidence of nonschool accomplishment	____	____	____	____	____	____
____	Nonacademic accomplishment	____	____	____	____	____	____
____	Reflections on student work, progress	____	____	____	____	____	____
____	Suggestions for future work	____	____	____	____	____	____
____	Critical or evaluative comments	____	____	____	____	____	____
____	Photos, audiotapes, videotapes	____	____	____	____	____	____
____	Transcript or grade list	____	____	____	____	____	____
____	Standardized test scores	____	____	____	____	____	____
____	Other	____	____	____	____	____	____
____	Other	____	____	____	____	____	____
____	Other	____	____	____	____	____	____

List required portfolio components.

List optional portfolio components.

Will student work entries have evaluative comments attached? _____

Will student work entries have reflective comments attached? _____

Will I create forms to be used for evaluative and/or reflective comments or not? _____

How often will the contents be reviewed and added or pruned? _____

How many pieces should be in the portfolio by the end of the course or year? _____

If a student and I (or others) disagree, how will the final decision regarding contents be made?

_____

I consider these portfolios/the portfolio process to be (check one): _____

_____ relatively unstructured _____ moderately structured _____ relatively structured

3. <u>Preparation.</u> **Will student work be collected in a preliminary folder from which portfolio contents will be selected?**

If yes, what will go into the preliminary folder?

__ All student work

__ Work in these subject or topical areas:

    a.

    b.

    c.

    d.

__ These kinds of student (individual or group) work:

    __ Tests

    __ Worksheets

    __ Writings, reports

    __ Drawings, diagrams, other artwork

    __ Photographs, audiotapes, videotapes of individual work or projects

    __ Photographs, audiotapes, videotapes of group work or projects

    __ Other:

        a.

        b.

        c.

        d.

__ Entries contributed by other persons (e.g., teacher, peers, parents), including:

    __ Descriptions and/or critiques of the student's in-school cognitive/academic accomplishments, progress, strengths and weaknesses.

        By whom? _____

    __ Descriptions and/or critiques of the student's out-of-school cognitive/academic accomplishments, progress, strengths and weaknesses.

        By whom? _____

    __ Descriptions and/or critiques of the student's nonacademic accomplishments, progress, strengths and weaknesses (e.g., group skills, persistence, strategies)

        By whom? _____

    __ List of grades

    __ Other:

        a.

        b.

        c.

        d.

If no, what will go into the portfolio (use questions above) and what will stay?

4. Portfolio organization. How will portfolio contents be organized?

___ By academic subject area
    ___ a different portfolio for each subject
    ___ one portfolio with sections for each subject

___ By topics within an academic subject area. List topics:
    a.
    b.
    c.
    d.

___ By type or work:
    ___ Students' best work (tests, papers, reports)
    ___ Unsuccessful products
    ___ Drafts as well as completed products
    ___ Required entries
    ___ Optional or nonrequired entries
    ___ Evidence of a range of accomplishment
    ___ Evidence of group work
    ___ Evidence of nonschool accomplishment
    ___ Nonacademic accomplishment
    ___ Reflections on student work, progress
    ___ Suggestions for future work
    ___ Critical or evaluative comments
    ___ Photos, audiotapes, videotapes
    ___ Transcript or grade list
    ___ Standardized test scores
    ___ Other
    ___ Other
    ___ Other

___ Chronologically to show progress over time
___ Work first, reflections/evaluations later
___ Reflections/evaluations attached to or accompanying work
___ Other:

5. <u>**Ownership, storage, access.**</u> **Who will own, store, give access to the portfolio?**

Who will own the portfolio?
__ student
__ teacher
__ school
    __ where the portfolio was created
    __ the student currently attends
__ other:
__ joint ownership
    __ student and teacher
    __ student and parents
    __ other:

Where will portfolios be stored during the school year?
__ preportfolio folders will be stored in the classroom at _____.
__ portfolios will be stored in the classroom at _____.
__ portfolios will be stored at school at _____.
__ students will keep portfolios at _____.

Where will portfolios be stored after the school year is over?
__ portfolios will be stored in the classroom at _____.
__ portfolios will be stored at school at _____.
__ students will keep portfolios at _____.

Who will have access to portfolios?
__ student
__ other students
__ teacher
__ other teachers
__ parents
__ counselors
__ administrators
    __ school
    __ district
    __ state
__ prospective employers
__ other:

Will the portfolio be transferred when the student leaves the school? How?

How will the student's right to privacy be protected?

5. Assessment. How will I use the portfolio to assess student achievement?

___ Will I use the portfolio to assess student achievement?
___ Will student work be judged holistically, using my intuitive expertise?
___ Will student work be judged analytically, using preset criteria and standards?
___ Will student goals, progress, and/or background be considered in judging work?
___ Will I describe and critique work? In writing? To be included in the portfolio?
___ Will I assign a grade to the portfolio as a whole?
___ Will I assign grades to portfolio entries?
___ Will I weight some entries or aspects more than others? If yes, which?
___ Will the student play a role in assessing his/her achievement?
___ Will others play a role in assessing student achievement? If yes, who?
___ How important will the evaluations of others be in comparison with my own?
___ How important will the portfolio be in my assessment of student achievement?
___ What other measures, if any, will I use to assess student achievement? List.
    a.
    b.
    c.

What criteria will be used to determine the quality of portfolios?
___ Completeness or thoroughness of information included
___ Sophistication of thought and work (depth of learning)
___ Variety of entries (breadth of learning)
___ Individual expression or creativity in entries or in the portfolio as a whole
___ Evidence of growth in knowledge and skills over time
___ Evidence of increased understanding, approach, or attitude over time
___ Evaluations of quality included with entries
___ Other:

Who will determine the criteria by which portfolios are assessed?
___ Individual teacher
___ Teachers as a group
___ Individual student
___ Students as a group
___ School administrators
___ District administrators
___ State administrators
___ Parents
___ Community
___ Assessment experts

What will I do if assessors disagree about grades or the quality of student work?
___ My assessment, as the teacher, will be the determining factor.
___ Assessors will have to resolve their disagreements and reach consensus.
___ I will average the grades or scores, but give my grade or score the most weight.
___ I will average the grades or scores, giving all the same weight.
___ Each assessor's judgment will become part of the record.
___ Other. Describe:

How often will the portfolio be reviewed and/or assessed? _____

7. <u>Reporting.</u> How will I use the portfolio to report student achievement?

Documentary reporting
___ I will use the portfolio itself to document student achievement.
___ I will issue written description and critique of the portfolio for student records.
    ___ my description and critique
    ___ the student's description and critique
    ___ others' descriptions and critiques
___ The portfolio will be graded. The grade will be part of the course grade.
___ Portfolio entries will be graded. The grades will be part of the course grade.
___ Other. Describe:

Those who will receive documentary reports of student achievement
___ The usual audiences: student, parents, school
___ And other audiences. List.
    a.
    b.
    c.
    d.

Public exhibiting
___ The school or class will display their portfolios publicly.
    where:
    when:
    invitations or publicity:
___ Students will display and describe or explain their portfolios publicly.
    where:
    when:
    invitations or publicity:
___ Student/parent consent will be secured before exhibit.

Archiving
___ Portfolios (or copies of portfolios) will be stored for future or historical purposes.
    ___ all portfolios
    ___ some portfolios
        ___ school or teacher selected
        ___ student selected
    ___ in the classroom
    ___ at the school
    ___ by the state
___ Student/parent consent will be secured before archiving.

3. Learning. **How will the portfolio inform teaching and curriculum development?**

What are my instructional goals?

a.

b.

c.

d.

Linking assessment to instruction in my class:

___ Is the portfolio used as evidence of meeting curriculum objectives?

___ Is the portfolio used as evidence of intellectual achievement, such as thinking skills, decision-making skills, coherence building, personalization of knowledge?

___ Will student interests, as evident in the portfolio, guide selection of new topics of learning?

___ Will student interests, as evident in the portfolio, guide selection of some new topics of learning?

___ Will student strengths, as evident in the portfolio, be considered in selecting new topics and projects?

___ Will student weaknesses, as evident in the portfolio, be addressed in selecting new topics and projects?

___ How else will I use portfolios to inform my teaching? Describe.

What are my school's/department's educational goals?

a.

b.

c.

d.

Linking assessment to schooling/the curriculum as a whole:

___ Is the portfolio used as evidence of meeting curriculum objectives?

___ Is the portfolio used as evidence of intellectual achievement, such as thinking skills, decision-making skills, coherence building, personalization of knowledge?

___ Will student achievement, as evident in the portfolio, guide advising of upcoming course selections?

___ How else will I/we use portfolios to inform curriculum planning? Describe.

Relating student work and portfolios directly to course or curriculum goals. List:

Learning Objectives	*Student Work*	*Portfolio Entries*
a.		
b.		
c.		
d.		

9. <u>**Staff development.**</u> **How will the faculty be prepared to use portfolios in our school?**

Who on our faculty will use portfolios?
__ all faculty
__ all faculty at _____ grade level/in _____ department
__ the following faculty members:

What kind of training or preparation would be useful?
__ Basic development information: definitions, types, purposes, contents of portfolios
__ Philosophy, rationale, issues
__ Assessment information: criteria, standards, methods, assessors
__ How-to information about portfolio creation and management
__ Examples of portfolio programs at other sites
__ Information about portfolio use at particular grade levels. List.
    a.
    b.
    c.
    d.
__ Information about portfolio use in particular subject areas. List.
    a.
    b.
    c.
    d.

Other:

__ We will not conduct a needs assessment to determine training foci.
__ We will conduct a needs assessment to determine training foci.
    Who will survey needs and concerns?
    When will the survey occur?
    When should training begin?
    When will portfolio implementation begin?

Training sources with contact information:

REFERENCES

Aiken, L. R. (1989). *Assessment of personality.* Boston: Allyn & Bacon.

Allina, A. (1991, March). *Beyond standardized tests: Admissions alternatives that work.* Cambridge, MA: National Center for Fair and Open Testing.

American Educational Research Association, American Psychological Association, & National Council on Measurement in Education. (1985). *Standards for educational and psychological testing.* Washington, DC: Author.

American Educational Research Association, American Psychological Association, & the National Council on Measurement in Education. (1998, March 23). *Standards for educational and psychological testing* [Draft]. Washington, DC: Author. Available: www.apa.org/science/standards.html

American Federation of Teachers, the National Council on Measurement in Education, & the National Education Association. (1990). *Standards for teacher competence in educational assessment of students.* Washington, DC: Author.

Anonymous Walden graduate. (1992, July 3). Old-fashioned ignorance. *Racine Journal-Times,* p. 6c.

Archbald, D. A., & Newmann, F. M. (1988). *Beyond standardized testing: Assessing authentic academic achievement in the secondary school.* Reston, VA: National Association of Secondary School Principals.

Archbald, D. A., & Newmann, F. M. (1992). Approaches to assessing academic achievement. In H. Berlak, F. M. Newmann, E. Adams, D. A. Archbald, T. Burgess, J. Raven, & T. A. Romberg, T*oward a new science of educational testing and assessment* (pp. 139-180). Albany: State University of New York Press.

Beckford, I. A., & Cooley, W. W. (1993, December). The racial achievement gap in Pennsylvania. *Pennsylvania Educational Policy Studies,* No. 18.

Bensman, D. (1995, April). *Learning to think well: The role of portfolio assessment in the education of Central Park East Secondary School graduates.* Paper presented at the annual meeting of the American Educational Research Association, San Francisco.

Berlak, H. (1992a). The need for a new science of assessment. In H. Berlak, F. M. Newmann, E. Adams, D. A. Archbald, T. Burgess, J. Raven, & T. A.

Romberg, *Toward a new science of educational testing and assessment* (pp. 1-22). Albany: State University of New York Press.

Berlak, H. (1992b). Toward the development of a new science of educational testing and assessment. In H. Berlak, F. M. Newmann, E. Adams, D. A. Archbald, T. Burgess, J. Raven, & T. A. Romberg, *Toward a new science of educational testing and assessment* (pp. 181-206). Albany: State University of New York Press.

Berliner, D. C., & Biddle, B. J. (1995). *The manufactured crisis: Myths, fraud, and the attack on America's public schools.* Reading, MA: Addison-Wesley.

Bloom, A. (1987). *The closing of the American mind: How higher education has failed democracy and impoverished the souls of today's students.* New York: Simon and Schuster.

Bloom, B. S., Englehart, M. D., Furst, G. J., Hill, W. H., & Krathwohl, D. R. (1956). *Taxonomy of educational objectives: Handbook I, The cognitive domain.* New York: David McKay.

Bond, L. A. (1994). *State student assessment programs database, 1992-93* [Draft]. Oak Brook, IL: Council of Chief State School Officers and the North Central Regional Educational Laboratory.

Bond, L. A., Braskamp, D., van der Ploeg, A., & Roeber, E. (1996). *State student assessment programs database, school year 1994-95.* Oak Brook, IL: Council of Chief State School Officers and the North Central Regional Educational Laboratory.

Bowman, C. M., & Peng, S. S. (1972). *A preliminary investigation of recent advanced psychology tests from the GRE program—An application of a cognitive classification system.* Unpublished ETS report. Princeton, NJ: Educational Testing Service.

Bransford, J. D. (1979). *Human cognition: Learning, understanding and remembering.* Belmont, CA: Wadsworth.

Brewer, R. (1991, June). *Portfolio assessment—Findings from research and practice.* Presentation to the Alternative Assessment Conference of the Education Commission of the States and the Colorado Department of Education, Breckenridge, CO.

Broadfoot, P. (Ed.). (1986). *Profiles and records of achievement: A review of issues and practice.* London: Cassell Education.

Broadfoot, P. (1996). Assessment and learning: Power or partnership? In H. Goldstein & T. Lewis (Eds.), *Assessment: Problems, developments and statistical issues* (pp. 21-40). New York: Wiley.

Broadfoot, P., James, M., McMeeking, S., Nuttall, D., & Stierer, B. (1988). *Records of achievement: Report of the national evaluation of pilot schemes.* London: Her Majesty's Stationery Office.

Bronfenbrenner, U. (1979). *The ecology of human development.* Cambridge, MA: Harvard University Press.

Brooks, A. P. (1998a, May 29). Policy flunks pupils in Waco. *Austin American-Statesman* [On-line]. Available: http://archives.statesman.com

Brooks, A. P. (1998b, June 10). Waco to fail large number of 1st-, 2nd-graders. *Austin American-Statesman* [On-line]. Available: http://archives.statesman.com

Burke, K. (1994). *The mindful school: How to assess authentic learning.* Palatine, IL: IRI/Skylight.

Burstein, L. (1991, April). *Performance assessment for accountability purposes: Taking the plunge and assessing the consequences.* Paper presented at the annual meeting of the American Educational Research Association, Chicago.

Burton, N. (1996). Have changes in the SAT affected women's mathematics performance? *Educational Measurement: Issues and Practice, 15*(4), 5-9.

Calandra, A. (1968, December 21). The barometer story. *Saturday Review,* p. 60.

Camp, R. (1990). Thinking together about portfolios. *Quarterly of the National Writing Project and the Center for the Study of Writing, 12*(2), 8-14, 27.

Cannell, J. J. (1987a). *Nationally normed elementary achievement testing in America's public schools: How all 50 states are above the national average.* Daniels, WV: Friends for Education.

Cannell, J. J. (1987b). Nationally normed elementary achievement testing in America's public schools: How all 50 states are above the national average. *Educational Measurement: Issues and Practice, 7*(2), 5-9.

Cohen, R. J., Montague, P., Nathanson, L. S., & Swerdlik, M. E. (1988). *Psychological testing: An introduction to tests and measurement.* Mountain View, CA: Mayfield.

Cole, D. J., Ryan, C. W., & Kick, F. (1995). *Portfolios across the curriculum and beyond.* Thousand Oaks, CA: Corwin.

Cole, N. S. (1988). A realist's appraisal of the prospects of unifying instruction and assessment. In *Proceedings of the invitational conference on assessment in the service of learning* (pp. 103-116). Princeton, NJ: Educational Testing Service.

College Board. (1990). *College bound seniors national report, 1990.* New York: Author.

Collins, J. (1997, October 27). Standards: The states go their own ways. *Time,* p. 75.

Colvin, R. L. (1997, December 31). Can essay tests really make the grade? *Los Angeles Times,* Valley Edition, pp. A1, 24-25.

Connell, W. F. (1980). *A history of education in the twentieth century world.* Canberra, Australia: Curriculum Development Centre.

Conoly, J. C., & Impara, J. C. (1995). *The twelfth mental measurements yearbook.* Lincoln: Buros Institute of Mental Measurements, University of Nebraska Press.

Cooley, W. W., & Bernauer, J. A. (1991). School comparisons in statewide testing programs. *Pennsylvania Educational Policy Studies,* No. 3.

Pittsburgh, PA: Learning and Development Center, Pittsburgh University School of Education.

Cronbach, L. J. (1988). Five perspectives on the validity argument. In H. Wainer & H. I. Braun (Eds.), *Test validity* (pp. 3-17). Hillsdale, NJ: Lawrence Erlbaum.

Cronbach, L. J., & Meehl, P. E. (1955). Construct validity in psychological tests. *Psychological Bulletin, 52,* 281-302.

Darling-Hammond, L. (1994). Performance-based assessment and educational equity. *Harvard Educational Review, 64*(1), 5-30.

Daugherty, R. (1995). *National curriculum assessment: A review of policy 1987-1994.* London: Falmer.

Debra P. v. Turlington, 564 F.Supp. 177, 179 (11 Ed. Law Rep. [893]) (M. D. Fla. 1983).

Delandshere, G., & Petrosky, A. R. (1994). Capturing teachers' knowledge: Performance assessment (a) and post-structuralist epistemology, (b) from a post-structuralist perspective, (c) and post-structuralism, (d) none of the above. *Educational Researcher, 23*(5), 11-18.

Delandshere, G., & Petrosky, A. R. (1998). Assessment of complex performances: Limitations of key measurement assumptions. *Educational Researcher, 27*(2), 14-24.

Dewey, J. (1909). *Moral principles in education.* Carbondale: Southern Illinois University Press.

Dewey, J. (1916). *Democracy and education: An introduction to the philosophy of education.* New York: Macmillan.

Edwards, T. M. (1998, June 15). Revolt of the gentry. *Time,* pp. 34-35.

Eisner, E. (1992, April). *National school reform: Seeking the silver bullet.* Paper presented at the annual meeting of the American Educational Research Association, San Francisco.

Eisner, E. (1993). Why standards may not improve schools. *Educational Leadership, 50*(5), 22-23.

Ennis, R. H. (1980). Presidential address: A conception of rational thinking. In J. Coombs (Ed.), *Philosophy of education 1979* (pp. 3-30). Bloomington, IL: Philosophy of Education Society.

Feldt, L. S., & Brennan, R. L. (1989). Reliability. In R. L. Linn (Ed.), *Educational measurement* (3rd ed., pp. 105-146). New York: American Council on Education, Macmillan.

Fisher, T. H., & Smith, J. (1991). Adventures in implementing a testing program. *Educational Measurement: Issues and Practice, 10*(1), 24-26.

Forte, L. V. (1991, April). Rite of passage puts teens to test. *Catalyst,* p. 5.

Frechtling, J. A. (1991). Performance assessment: Moonstruck or the real thing? *Educational Measurement: Issues and Practice, 10*(4), 23-25.

Frederiksen, J. R., & Collins, A. (1989). A systems approach to educational testing. *Educational Researcher, 18*(9), 27-32.

Fuhrman, S. H., & Elmore, R. F. (1990). Understanding local control in the wake of state education reform. *Educational Evaluation and Policy Analysis, 12*(1), 82-96.

Gardner, H. (1983). *Frames of mind: The theory of multiple intelligences.* New York: Basic Books.

Gitomer, D. H. (1993). Performance assessment and educational measurement. In R. E. Bennett & W. C. Ward (Eds.), *Construction versus choice in cognitive measurement* (pp. 241-263). Hillsdale, NJ: Lawrence Erlbaum.

Glaberson, W. (1989, February 4). U.S. court says awards based on S.A.T.'s are unfair to girls. *New York Times,* pp. 1, 50.

GOALS 2000: Educate America Act of 1994, Public Law 103-227, Sec. 1 et seq. 108 Stat. 125 (1994).

Gonzalez, E. (1998). *A study of colonia students in a southwest Texas school: Lessons for educators.* Unpublished doctoral dissertation, Indiana University, Bloomington.

Grades. (1986, June 1). *Milwaukee Journal,* p. 8.

Gray, J. (1996). The use of assessment to compare institutions. In H. Goldstein & T. Lewis (Eds.), *Assessment: Problems, developments and statistical issues* (pp. 121-133). New York: Wiley.

Green, S. W. (1998). *How to prepare for the SAT I* (20th ed.). Hauppauge, NY: Barrons.

Gronlund, N. E. (1993). *How to make achievement tests and assessments* (5th ed.). Boston: Allyn & Bacon.

Haertel, E. H., & Mullis, I. V. S. (1996). The evolution of the National Assessment of Educational Progress: Coherence with best practice. In J. B. Baron & D. P. Wolf (Eds.), *Performance-based student assessment: Challenges and possibilities* (pp. 287-304). Chicago: National Society for the Study of Education, University of Chicago Press.

Haladyna, T. M., Nolen, S. B., & Haas, N. S. (1991). Raising standardized achievement test scores and the origins of test score pollution. *Educational Researcher, 20*(5), 2-7.

Hambleton, R., Jaeger, R., Koretz, D., Linn, R. L., Millman, J., & Phillips, S. E. (1995). *Technical review of the Kentucky Instructional Results Information System (KIRIS), 1991-94.* Frankfort: Office of Educational Accountability of the Kentucky General Assembly.

Hansen, L. (in preparation). *The effects of educational system policies and practices on an innovative arts-and-education program.* Unpublished doctoral dissertation, Indiana University, Bloomington.

Harvard Project Zero. (1998, Fall). Arts education partnerships for in-depth study. *Arts Survive! News.* Cambridge, MA: Author.

Hill, R., & Hoover, H. D. (1991, June). *Authenticity, validity and efficiency: When must we use authentic measures? When needn't we? When are we best and least well served by conventional measures?* Presentation to the Alternative Assessment Conference of the Education Commission of the States and the Colorado Department of Education, Breckenridge, CO.

Hillocks, G. (1997, March). *How state mandatory assessment simplifies writing instruction in Illinois and Texas.* Paper presented at the annual meeting of the American Educational Research Association, Chicago.

Hirsch, E. D., Jr. (1987). *Cultural literacy.* Boston: Houghton-Mifflin.

Hopkins, K. D., Stanley, J. C., & Hopkins, B. R. (1990). *Educational and psychological measurement and evaluation.* Boston: Allyn & Bacon.

House, E. (1996). A framework for appraising educational reforms. *Educational Researcher, 25*(7), 6-14.

Illinois State Board of Education, School and Student Assessment Section. (1995, January). *Assessment handbook: A guide for developing assessment programs in Illinois schools.* Springfield: Author.

Impara, J., & Plake, B. (1997, March). *Standard setting: Variation on a theme by Anghoff.* Paper presented at the annual meeting of the American Educational Research Association, Chicago.

Indiana Education Policy Center. (1994). *Education in Indiana: An overview.* Bloomington: Indiana Education Policy Center, School of Education.

Jaeger, R. M. (1991). Legislative perspectives on statewide testing. *Phi Delta Kappan, 73,* 239-242.

Kane, M. (1994). Validating the performance standards associated with passing scores. *Review of Educational Research, 64*(3), 425-561.

Kentucky Department of Education. (1994). *Measuring up!* [Brochure]. Frankfort: Author.

Koretz, D. (1992). *The reliability of scores from the 1992 Vermont portfolio assessment program: Interim report* (Tech. Rep. No. 355). Los Angeles: UCLA Center for the Study of Evaluation.

Koretz, D. (1993, April). *Portfolio assessment: Rhetoric meets the reality of data.* Paper presented at the annual meeting of the American Educational Research Association, Atlanta, GA.

Koretz, D., Stecher, B., Klein, S., & McCaffrey, D. (1994). The Vermont portfolio assessment program: Findings and implications. *Educational Measurement: Issues and Practice, 13*(3), 5-16.

Kozol, J. (1992). *Savage inequalities: Children in America's schools.* New York: HarperPerennial.

Kozol, J. (1995). *Amazing grace: The lives of children and the conscience of a nation.* New York: Crown.

Kubiszyn, T., & Borich, G. (1996). *Educational testing and measurement: Classroom application and practice* (5th ed.). New York: HarperCollins.

Kuhn, T. (1962). *The structure of scientific revolutions.* Princeton, NJ: Princeton University Press.

Lapointe, A. E. (1986). Testing in the USA. In D. Nuttall (Ed.), *Assessing educational achievement* (pp. 114-124). London: Falmer.

Lather, P. (1986). Issues of validity in openly ideological research: Between a rock and a soft place. *Interchange, 17,* 63-84.

Law, B. (1984). *Uses and abuses of profiling.* London: Harper & Row.

Lawton, M. (1997, August 6). Feds position national tests on fast track. *Education Week, 16*(41), 1, 34-35.

Lazarovici, L. (1997, August 28). ED would let NAGB oversee voluntary national tests. *Education Daily, 30*(167), 1-2.

LeMahieu, P. (1993, April). *Portfolio assessment: Rhetoric meets the reality of data.* Paper presented at the annual meeting of the American Educational Research Association, Atlanta, GA.

LeMahieu, P., & Eresh, J. T. (1996). Coherence, comprehensiveness, and capacity in assessment systems: The Pittsburgh experience. In J. B. Baron & D. P. Wolf (Eds.). *Performance-based student assessment: Challenges and possibilities* (pp. 125-142). Chicago: National Society for the Study of Education, University of Chicago Press.

Lemire, C. (1998, May 14). Court rejects TAAS score dispute. *Austin American-Statesman.* [On-line]. (Available: http://archives.statesman.com)

Lichota, A. (1981, June 28). Gains expected in skills test. *New York Times,* p. 13.

Lightfoot-Clark, R. (1997, May 7). Test gender gaps may hinge on after-school activities. *Education Daily, 30*(88), 1, 3.

Linn, R. L. (1994, November). *Assessment-based reform: Challenges to educational measurement.* First annual William H. Angoff Memorial Lecture presented at Educational Testing Service, Princeton, NJ.

Linn, R. L. (1997, March). *Measuring school performance: Is "percents of students reading standards" the most accurate statistic?* [Discussant]. Paper presented at the annual meeting of the American Educational Research Association, Chicago.

Linn, R. L., Baker, E. L., & Dunbar, S. B. (1991). Complex, performance-based assessment: Expectations and validation criteria. *Educational Researcher, 20*(8), 15-21.

Mabry, L. (1992a, April). *Empirical evidence of validity and reliability in measuring student achievement via alternative methods.* Paper presented at the annual meeting of the American Educational Research Association, San Francisco.

Mabry, L. (1992b). Twenty years of alternative assessment at an American high school. *The School Administrator, 11*(49), 12-13.

Mabry, L. (1995a). *Naturally occurring reliability.* Paper presented at the annual meeting of the American Educational Research Association, San Francisco.

Mabry, L. (1995b). One small LEAP: A case study of the Lake View Education and Arts Partnership. In North Central Regional Educational Laboratory, *Chicago Arts Partnerships in Education: Final technical evaluation report, Year 1.* Oak Brook, IL: North Central Regional Educational Laboratory.

Mabry, L. (1995c). *Performance assessment and inferences of achievement.* Unpublished doctoral dissertation, University of Illinois at Urbana-Champaign.

Mabry, L. (1996). Assessment at Santana Math and Science Academy. In R. Stake, T. Souchet, R. Clift, L. Mabry, M. M. Basi, M. S. Whiteaker, C. A. Mills & T. Dunbar, *School improvement: Facilitating teacher professional development in Chicago school reform* (pp. 137-180). Urbana: Center for Instructional Research and Curriculum Evaluation, University of Illinois.

Mabry, L. (1997a). A dramatic difference in education in Chicago. *Stage of the Art, 9*(3), 17-22.

Mabry, L. (1997b). *State-mandated performance assessment: A research report to the Proffitt Foundation.* Unpublished report. Bloomington: Indiana University.

Mabry, L. (1997c). *Year 1 evaluation report: Inter-Campus Enhancement of Language Minority Teacher Recruitment and Bilingual Education program.* Bloomington: Indiana University.

Mabry, L. (1998). A forward LEAP: A study of the involvement of Beacon Street Art Gallery and Theatre in the Lake View Education and Arts Partnership. In D. Boughton & K. G. Congdon (Eds.), *Advances in program evaluation: Vol. 4. Evaluating art education programs in community centers: International perspectives on problems of conception and practice.* Greenwich, CT: JAI.

Mabry, L. (1999). Writing to the rubric: Lingering effects of traditional standardized testing on direct writing assessment. *Phi Delta Kappan, 80*(9), 673-679.

Mabry, L. (in preparation-a). *Local administration of state-mandated performance assessments.*

Mabry, L. (in preparation-b). *Personalized assessment of student achievement at Pan Terra High School.*

Mabry, L., & Daytner, K. G. (1997, March). *State-mandated performance assessment.* Paper presented at the annual meeting of the American Educational Research Association, Chicago.

Mabry, L., Daytner, K., & Aldarondo, J. (1999). *Local administration of state-mandated performance assessments in Indiana, Michigan, and Pennsylvania.* Research report to the Proffitt Foundation. Bloomington: Indiana University.

Mabry, L., & Gonzales, E. (in preparation). *State testing and culturally appropriate teaching: Conflict of interests.*

Madaus, G. F. (1991). The effects of important tests on students. *Phi Delta Kappan, 73*(3), 226-231.

Madaus, G. F., & Raczek, A. E. (1996). The extent and growth of educational testing in the United States: 1956-1994. In H. Goldstein & T. Lewis (Eds.), *Assessment: Problems, developments and statistical issues* (pp. 145-165). New York: Wiley.

Madaus, G. F., Scriven, M.S., & Stufflebeam, D. L. (Eds.). (1987). *Evaluation models: Viewpoints on educational and human services evaluation.* Boson: Kluwer-Nijhoff.

Mann, H. (1848). *Twelfth annual report of Horace Mann as secretary of Massachusetts State Board of Education.* Available: http://www.tncrimlaw.com/civil_bible/horace_mann.htm

Manzo, K. K. (1997, May 28). U.S. falls short in 4-nation study of math tests. *Education Week.*

Margolis, M. J., De Champlain, A. F., & Klass, D. J. (1998, April). *Comparing alternative procedures for scoring a performance assessment of physicians' clinical skills.* Paper presented at the annual meeting of the National Council on Measurement in Education, San Diego, CA.

Martinson, T. H. (1997). *GMAT: With computer adaptive tests on disk.* New York: Macmillan/Arco.

Maslow, A. H. (1970). *Motivation and personality* (2nd ed.). New York: Harper & Row.

Massell, D., Kirst, M., & Hoppe, M. (1997, March). *Persistence and change: Standards-based systemic reform in nine states.* CPRE Policy Briefs, RB-21. Philadelphia: Consortium for Policy Research in Education.

McAllister, P. H. (1991). Overview of state legislation to regulate standardized testing. *Educational Measurement: Issues and Practice, 10*(4), 19-22.

McLaughlin, M. S. (1991). Test-based accountability as a reform strategy. *Phi Delta Kappan, 73*(3), 248-252.

McLean, L. D. (1996). Large-scale assessment programmes in different countries and international comparisons. In H. Goldstein & T. Lewis (Eds.), *Assessment: Problems, developments and statistical issues* (pp. 189-207). New York: Wiley.

Meier, D. (1983). "Getting tough" in the schools: A critique of the conservative prescription. *Dissent,* pp. 61-70.

Messick, S. (1975). The standard problem: Meaning and values in measurement and evaluation. *American Psychologist, 30*(10), 955-966.

Messick, S. (1989). Validity. In R. L. Linn (Ed.), *Educational measurement* (3rd ed., pp. 13-103). New York: American Council on Education, Macmillan.

Moss, P. A. (1992). Shifting conceptions of validity in educational measurement: Implications for performance assessment. *Review of Educational Research, 62*(3), 229-258.

Moss, P. A. (1994). Can there be validity without reliability? *Educational Researcher, 23*(2), 5-12.

National Center for Fair and Open Testing. (1994). *K-12 testing fact sheet.* Cambridge, MA: Author. (ERIC Document Reproduction Service No. ED 352 376)

National Commission on Excellence in Education. (1983). *A nation at risk: The imperative for educational reform.* Washington, DC: Government Printing Office.

National Council of Teachers of Mathematics. (1989). *Curriculum and evaluation standards for school mathematics.* Reston, VA: Author.

National Council on Measurement in Education, American Educational Research Association. (1995). *Code of professional responsibility in educational assessment.* Washington, DC: Author.

National Education Goals Panel. (1993, 1994, & 1995). *The National Education Goals report.* Washington, DC: Government Printing Office.

Nolen, S. B., Haladyna, T. M., & Haas, N. S. (1992). Uses and abuses of achievement test scores. *Educational Measurement: Issues and Practice, 11*(2), 9-15.

O'Neil, J. (1993). On the New Standards Project: A conversation with Lauren Resnick and Warren Simmons. *Educational Leadership,*50 (5), 17-21.

Owen, D. (1985). *None of the above.* Boston: Houghton-Mifflin.

Paris, S. G., Lawton, T. A., Turner, J. C., & Roth, J. L. (1991). A developmental perspective on standardized achievement testing. *Educational Researcher, 20*(5), 12-20.

Parker, J. (1991, May). *A history of Walden III and R.O.P.E.* Presentation to the meeting of the Inquiry Committee for Alternative Assessment, Racine Unified School District, Racine, WI.

Paulson, F. L., & Paulson, P. R. (1991). *The ins and outs of using portfolios to assess performance.* Paper presented at the annual meeting of the National Council on Measurement in Education, Chicago.

Paulson, F. L., Paulson, P. R., & Meyer, C. A. (1991). What makes a portfolio a portfolio? *Educational Leadership, 48*(5), 60-63.

Peter Dalton v. Educational Testing Service. 87 NY 2d 384, 633 N.E. 2d 289, 639 N.Y.S. 2d 977 (1995).

Phillips, S. E. (1993). Legal issues in performance assessment. *Education Law Quarterly, 2*(2), 329-358.

Piaget, J. (1955). *The language and thought of the child.* New York: World.

Porter, A. (1995). The uses and misuses of opportunity-to-learn standards. *Educational Researcher, 24*(1), 21-27.

Rabinow, P. (Ed.). (1984). *The Foucault reader.* New York: Pantheon.

Racine Unified School District. (1990a). *Grad survey report, class of 1989.* Racine, WI: Author.

Racine Unified School District. (1990b). *Secondary test results and related school factors, 1989-1990.* Racine, WI: Author.

Ratnesar, R. (1998, September 14). Lost in the middle. *Time,* pp. 60-62, 64.

Raven, J. (1992). A model of competence, motivation, and behavior, and a paradigm for assessment. In H. Berlak, F. M. Newmann, E. Adams, D. A. Archbald, T. Burgess, J. Raven, & T. A. Romberg, *Toward a new science of educational testing and assessment* (pp. 85-116). Albany: State University of New York Press.

Resnick, L. B., & Resnick, D. P. (1992). Assessing the thinking curriculum: New tools for education reform. In B. R. Gifford & M. C. O'Connor (Eds.), *Future assessments: Changing views of aptitude, achievement, and instruction* (pp. 37-75). Boston: Kluwer Academic.

Rhode Island State Assessment Program. (1996). *1996 mathematics assessment: A guide to interpretation.* Providence: Author.

Rosser, P. (1987). *Sex bias in college admissions tests: Why women lose out* (2nd ed.). Cambridge, MA: National Center for Fair and Open Testing.

Rothman, R. (1992, August 5). Auditors help Pittsburgh make sure its portfolio assessment measures up. *Education Week,* pp. 1, 27-29.

Rugg, H., & Schumaker, A. (1928). *The child-centered school.* New York: World Book Co.

Rumelhart, D., & Norman, D. (1978). Accretion, tuning and restructuring: Three modes of learning. In J. W. Cotton & R. Klatzky (Eds.), *Semantic factors in cognition.* Hillsdale, NJ: Lawrence Erlbaum.

Schlesinger, A. M., Jr. (1993). *The disuniting of America: Reflections on a multicultural society.* New York: Norton.

Schön, D. A. (1995, November/December). Knowing-in-action: The new scholarship requires a new epistemology. *Change, 27,* 27-34.

Scriven, M. (1990). Beyond formative and summative. In M. McLaughlin & D. Phillips (Eds.), *Evaluation and education at quarter century* (pp. 19-64). Chicago: University of Chicago/National Society for the Study of Education.

Scriven, M. (1991). *Evaluation thesaurus* (4th ed.) Newbury Park, CA: Sage.

Shepard, L. A. (1991). Psychometricians' beliefs about learning influence testing. *Educational Researcher, 20*(7), 2-16.

Shepard, L. A., & Dougherty, K. C. (1991, April). *Effects of high stakes testing on instruction.* Paper presented at the annual meeting of the American Educational Research Association, Chicago.

Shepard, L. A., & Smith, M. L. (1988). Escalating academic demand in kindergarten: Counterproductive policies. *Elementary School Journal, 89*(2), 135-145.

Sixty years of idiocy is enough. (1987). *FairTest Examiner, 1*(1), 1.

Sizer, T. R. (1984). *Horace's compromise: The dilemma of the American high school.* Boston: Houghton-Mifflin.

Skinner, B. F. (1931). The concept of the reflex in the description of behavior. *Journal of General Psychology, 5,* 427-458.

Skinner, B. F. (1938). *The behavior of organisms: An experimental analysis.* Englewood Cliffs, NJ: Prentice Hall.

Smith, M. L. (1991). Put to the test: The effects of external testing on teachers. *Educational Researcher, 20*(5), 8-11.

Smith, M. L., & Rottenberg, C. (1991). Unintended consequences of external testing in elementary schools. *Educational Measurement: Issues and Practice, 10*(4), 7-11.

Spring, J. (1976). *The sorting machine.* New York: David McKay.

St. Louis Teachers Union v. St. Louis Board of Education, 652 F. Supp. 425 [37 Ed. Law Rep. [798]] (E.D. Mo. 1987).

Stake, R. E. (1991). *The invalidity of standardized testing for measuring mathematics achievement.* Monograph commissioned by the National

Center for Research on Mathematical Sciences Education, University of Wisconsin, Madison.

Stiggins, R. J., & Conklin, N. F. (1992). *In teachers' hands: Investigating the practices of classroom assessment.* Albany: State University of New York Press.

Stronach, I., & Maclure, M. (1996). Mobilizing meaning, demobilizing critique? Dilemmas in the deconstruction of educational discourse. *Cultural Studies, 1,* 259-276.

Suburban students gaining strength at UW–M. (1981, April). *Milwaukee Journal,* p. 2.

Sutherland, G. (1996). Assessment: Some historical perspectives. In H. Goldstein & T. Lewis (Eds.), *Assessment: Problems, developments and statistical issues* (pp. 9-20). New York: Wiley.

Texas school ties promotion solely to state test scores. (1998, June 3). *Education Daily,* p. 5.

Thorndike, E. L. (1921). Measurement in education. *Teachers College Record, 22*(5), 371-397.

Très-Brevig, M. da P. (1993). *Effects of implementation of assessment policy on staff practices at a state department of education.* Unpublished doctoral dissertation, University of Illinois at Urbana-Champaign.

U.S. General Accounting Office. (1993). *Student testing: Current extent and expenditures, with cost estimates for a national examination* (Report No. GAO/PEMD-93-8). Washington, DC: Author.

Vermont Department of Education. (1991). *Vermont's assessment program.* Montpelier: Author.

Viadero, D. (1997, June 4). Panel faces challenges in drafting blueprint for 1st national tests. *Education Week.*

Vygotsky, L. S. (1978). *Mind in society: The development of higher mental process.* Cambridge, MA: Harvard University Press.

Wainer, H., & Thissen, D. (1994). On examinee choice in educational testing. *Review of Educational Research, 64*(1), 159-195.

Wiggins, G. (1989). A true test: Toward more authentic and equitable assessment. *Phi Delta Kappan, 70*(9), 703-713.

Wiggins, G. (1991). Standards, not standardization: Evoking quality student work. *Educational Leadership, 48*(5), 18-25.

Wiggins, G. (1993). *Assessing student performance.* San Francisco: Jossey-Bass.

Wiggins. G. (1998). *Educative assessment.* San Francisco: Jossey-Bass.

Wilson, B. L., & Corbett, D. (1989). *Two state minimum competency testing programs and their effects on curriculum and instruction.* Philadelphia: Research for Better Schools.

Wisconsin Department of Public Instruction. (1995-1996). *Wisconsin writing assessment: Content and scoring criteria.* Madison: Author.

Wolf, A. (1993). *Assessment issues and problems in a criterion-based system.* London: Further Education Unit.

Wolf, D., Bixby, J., Glenn, J., III, & Gardner, H. (1991). To use their minds well: Investigating new forms of student assessment. In G. Grant (Ed.), *Review of research in education* (Vol. 17, pp. 31-74). Washington, DC: American Educational Research Association.

Wolf, D. P. (1989). Portfolio assessment: Sampling student work. *Educational Leadership, 46*(7), 35-39.

Wood, R. (1990). The agenda for educational measurement. In T. Horton (Ed.), *Assessment debates* (pp. 48-56). London: Hodder & Stoughton.

Worthen, B. R., Borg, W. R., & White, K. R. (1993). *Measurement and evaluation in the schools.* New York: Longman.

Worthen, B. R., Sanders, J. R., & Fitzpatrick, J. L. (1997). *Program evaluation: Alternative approaches and practical guidelines* (2nd ed.). New York: Longman.

Yen, W. M. (1997, March). *Measuring school performance: Is "percents of students reading standards" the most accurate statistic?* Paper presented at the annual meeting of the American Educational Research Association, Chicago.

INDEX

CORWIN
PRESS

The Corwin Press logo—a raven striding across an open book—represents the happy union of courage and learning. We are a professional-level publisher of books and journals for K–12 educators, and we are committed to creating and providing resources that embody these qualities. Corwin's motto is "Success for All Learners."

**CORWIN
PRESS**

The Corwin Press logo—a raven striding across an open book—represents the happy union of courage and learning. We are a professional-level publisher of books and journals for K–12 educators, and we are committed to creating and providing resources that embody these qualities. Corwin's motto is "Success for All Learners."

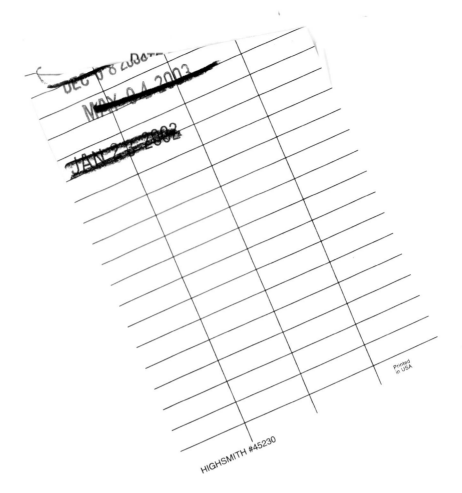